Home

Home

Richard Reitz

iUniverse, Inc.

New York Lincoln Shanghai

Home

iUniverse books may be ordered through booksellers or by contacting:

iUniverse
2021 Pine Lake Road, Suite 100
Lincoln, NE 68512
www.iuniverse.com
1-800-Authors (1-800-288-4677)

ISBN: 0-595-34012-1

Printed in the United States of America

For
Phyllis
Jill
Mike
Rosalee
Tim

And
thanks to Jerry for his cheerful and careful first read.

Contents

Preface

This is the story of growing and growing up in a place where human beings made a hard land home, a place of profound trust and security, space and responsibility. It celebrates family, the family of father and mother, the extended family of uncles and aunts and grandparents, the larger family of community, molded by the land and weather and time, yet never reduced by necessity into confusing making a living with making a life. It is about living in an agrarian world of the 30's and 40's, with all the usual uncertainties connected with crops and animal husbandry, and all the certainties of decent persons sharing a common endeavor, living close to the land and animals and each other. It is told quietly, respectfully, with no pretense of romantic or narrative embellishment.

A common denominator is hard, physical labor handled with the competence and grace of necessity and opportunity rather than the demands of hardship—handled so well that good times and leisure seem part of a seamless whole, no one, nothing, left out, all things part of the scheme, so that no other environment ever seems so complete and secure, no other place so reliable as to be called home.

Except for the names of my family, many names have been changed. I hated to do this. These persons are real to me: when I wrote about them I used their real names so that I could see them clearly. Later, I changed them. I do not know whether many of them are alive or dead, but I would not risk giving offense. They were all important and special to me once. In a sense, all of them still are.

Everything described is as real as I can remember though, or course, memory is never perfect. Still, I have not tried to fill in gaps with invention, reasonable inference maybe, but not invention. Too, I wanted this to be something more than reminiscence. I wanted to tell the story of persons, times, and places that might not otherwise be told, for the persons involved lived modest lives and had modest expectations. And I wanted to tell the story of a lucky growing up: a time of space and love and responsibility, a time of unbelievable and irretrievable security. One's parents were always there and always had time to teach and to listen. If we talked so much it is because we knew we had an audience. If we needed help it was there without question. If we hurt, the sympathy was real.

We live now in a time when the only truth is thought to be negative, when one should be certain to emphasize evils: a child working must be abused; another ethnicity is perforce the subject of bias and exploitation; living away from some kind of paternalistic safety net is to be "underprivileged," a word that by itself demonstrates a pathetic ignorance of what "privilege" has always meant. If a woman takes care of a family and a home without the prestige of a "career," she must be a victim of male "chauvinism," (another word whose meaning has been distorted). Even that neutral or generic gender which language has always used is called into question. In order not to offend anyone, one cannot risk the truth anymore, even when it is positive.

It may come as a shock to our contemporary professional pessimists (and I hope it does) to know that most humans, given half a chance, are creatures of good will, at least most humans left to their own care and responsibility; that even selfishness and self-aggrandizement have their limitations; that even the most realistic and cynical of us must admit to unexpected exception. At the very least, decency is always a possibility.

And so, finally, I celebrate the persons and places of our lives and livelihoods, the fields and meadows, the hills and valleys, the two special rivers, the small towns and farmsteads, the ranch yards—and the animals.

I do not pretend that I have done any of them justice, the persons, the places, or the animals. I had my own world to live in too and have no doubt that I saw only a hill or two in the landscape that made up our lives and understood even less; yet, given what I remember, I do not subscribe to the pejorative "nobody's perfect," having never seen perfection except as a philosophical theory or as short-hand for someone's arbitrary standards: so far as I am concerned, as humans, the humans of my experience were perfect—all of them, without exception. That's how it should be. That's how it was.

Southsiders

In March the mallards came, wedges and skeins with endless soft quacks and whistling wings against the dusk and afterglow and stars, or they came on cloudy afternoons above the mixed mud and melting snow of barbed wired fencerows. In the waning light the flocks flew closer to the damp earth and began breaking into small circling groups to land in old cornstalks, their numbers ever increasing until the sky was empty but the fields were full of muted and private chuckles and clucks and quacks as the birds waddled in a steady, seemingly organized direction to glean the kernels harvest had missed. If disturbed they rose in numbers that thickened the horizon to black with a noise that in those days was likened to the sound of a hundred freight trains pulled by steam-powered locomotives, if one could imagine a hundred freight trains pulled by steam-powered locomotives together on a hundred tracks.

As a boy then I often walked the three and a half miles home after school with my face to the sky to watch, or my ear to listen, the lines of mallards muttering overhead; and sometimes getting home took a long time as I detoured across the fields to sit in the fencerows, on the cleaner snow, and looked and listened and sniffed; for the fecund scent of March was as distinctive and memorable as were those glorious, flashing, whistling wings. There were late evenings when I went out with an old .22 rifle and tried to bring a bird down, to get a closer look at the fluorescent green head and the white bordered blue speculum, though there was no season in March. Once I expended a whole box of .22's, but usually I had only one or two opportunities, if trying to hit a flying duck with a rifle can be considered an opportunity. These were not very serious attempts, for I did not like to compromise those magical evenings of wild sound just above my head with the sharp report of the little rifle, though in reality .22's make only modest noise when fired against the sky. I never hit anything, but it gave me a sense of closer participation in that magnificent outdoor spectacle. Mostly, I just stood in the cold darkness, listening, and looking up at early stars for the source of the quick whistling wings.

Mainly I remember being most alive and happiest in March, somewhere between winter and spring, at dusk, with the scent of the dark wet earth in my nostrils and the subtle staccato whistling of duck wings overhead. Everything before and after relates to that. Then, one was connected to, part of, earth itself. I know this to be true of boys carrying old .22 rifles through the afterglow toward the shelterbelt and the light in the kitchen window. Thinking of this now I know I can remember this in detail at least a dozen times and ways; but it is always part of the consciousness of a boy become a man, especially a country boy who had access to space and uncluttered dark skies full of waterfowl and the freedom to move without reference to anything but fences and cornstalks and stars.

That time and place and awareness measures dreams realized and unrealized; it is the measure of what forever after has held importance—assessing success or failure, intention and result. It not only hints at what is important but defines what is appropriate also. It is the defining reminiscence, boy to man to the end of it, for it includes outdoors and indoors, earth, sky, and family. This is where I began, *in medias res as* I think of it now.

Though we are creatures of memory, prisoners of memory, one might say, important memories are not chronological. What is most memorable is not neatly arranged according to time, nor does the sense of what is most important in the creation of one's intellect or character lend itself to any easy or neat assembly. An internal hierarky will have to do the arrangements and assign credit where due. Perhaps some useful order is found in relating oneself and others to place. Most of us seem to remain more or less territorial all our lives. *Where are you from?*, we say. We were "southsiders" when the mallards flew; before that were the third and second and first farms—*in medias res* back in time to place; perhaps that's as close to the chronological as memory works, and what happens before and after the middle, when we have become ourselves, has its use as perspective in the discovery of just where our real beginnings began.

Where we were from as southsiders was in the shortgrass prairie become a mixture of pasture and dry-land farms south of the South Platte in western Nebraska, a treeless country except for shelterbelts planted by the people who lived there. It was a land that alternated between the rolling and the flat, with areas of deep topsoil and areas of hills too sandy to plow. It was the sandy areas, usually hills, that were left to pasture. Naturally, some of the sandy areas that shouldn't have been plowed, were; and we had two such a places on our farm. One was disconnected from the major pasture, steep and sandy, but for some reason it was plowed shortly after we came there to live. Plowing took special plows to turn over the millennia-created old grass, the black root soil, as it was called. Such soil was always rich at first, but if it was over-layment for sandy soil would eventually blow or had to be tilled in alternating strips to minimize the wind damage. The hills there were so steep that you thought your tractor would turn over on a side hill. We strip farmed it at first, then planted alfalfa to hold the soil. Dry land alfalfa didn't grow very tall, but it held the soil. Like so much of that country, it should never have been plowed. I don't know whose decision it was to break it up. The other sandy place was a hilltop in an otherwise productive field. We eventually planted it in alfalfa too.

The major pasture bordered the farmstead on the north and was divided by a road, but we had a tunnel under the road ("underpass") that allowed the stock to go from the "south pasture" to the "north pasture" at will. The livestock had to come through the south pasture for water. The rest of the farm consisted of good, level to fairly level farm land with deep, rich, black topsoil. The fences all ran north-south or east-west and you could travel for hundreds of miles east and south and west and find the same patterns of field and pastures and farmsteads with shelterbelts; but north of the Plattes were the sandhills, stretching all the way to South Dakota. If you were to draw a line on a map straight north of our place, you could probably get all the way to the Arctic Circle without hitting a major town; if you went south you might hit something in Mexico somewhere. But you could see something of the shortgrass prairie on the farm's southern border, where there was a lane that acted as a simple two-track road, and the grass had never been touched. It is big, empty country. For a boy the biannual mallards were a main relief from the monotony of fields and fences that seemed to go on forever.

More important even than place, of course, is family, especially a country family who didn't have to keep their voices down or pull their shades at night. Throughout those great spring migrations my family and I, especially my father and I, watched and listened and marveled, knowing that the huge flocks would reappear in the fall, when we could hunt. When I got old enough, I would go out before daylight and sit with my father's Winchester shotgun across my lap in the cornfield the ducks were using, shoot a brace at dawn, and still have time to drive to town for school.

In the earlier years of the March mallards there was a war, which was good for the birds but bad for boys who needed shotgun shells, especially boys considered too young for the regular gauges, which I was in those first years as a southsider. Some ammunition was on occasion available for the larger gauges, but my father was always conservative—too conservative in my eyes—when it came to letting me shoot a shotgun bigger than the .410 he showed up with one day.

The war continued until I was in high school, a time of "Steve Canyon" and of uniformed young men in jeeps selling war bonds, and other young men just a little too young to go to war doodling P-40's, and, before it was all over, P-51's and B-17's, beside notes on American history in ring binders, or who delighted in cartoons showing things like Der Fuerer being scrubbed on a washboard with the cutline: "all washed up and ready to hang."

Migrating mallards were beyond all that, coming and going in the most ancient of ways, a connection to a kind of sanity, to an ineluctable, almost holy, peace—even to a boy, perhaps especially to a boy whose ears were full of war and had been full of war already for two or three years.

The ducks came after the bomb that changed all things too. Then, if the lagoons—our name for what were at other places called potholes—were full, (those low places in the fields of cornstalks and wheat stubble that filled with water when there was enough snow melt or rain), the mallards would cover them black at night; and just once in those years I remember my father taking his 16-gauge out on a black night and shooting three times into the dark mass as it thundered skyward. He did it mainly for me as I was, with the help of the J.W. Elwood School of Taxidermy, a learn-by-mail school based in Omaha, learning to mount birds; and I needed a practice bird. (Of course we ate the birds I skinned. Wasting animals was always unthinkable.) I wanted to have the birds I admired where I could see them regularly, and taxidermy seemed the obvious answer. The fourteen dollars I was investing for the series of lessons, delivered in small, illustrated booklets every month, was a significant commitment for a thirteen year old at that time. I didn't know then how quickly I would earn my tuition back with my first two custom jobs, a pheasant for someone in town and then a white dove for a women's organization, which needed it as a symbol for some kind of ceremony. The most interesting thing about the white dove commission was that the women did not provide the dove. It must have been providence that sent an all-white pigeon to the ridge of our barn roof only a day or two after getting that assignment—we did not raise pigeons. The bird probably came from the Mennonite community to the west. I had seen pigeons there. My father collected the pigeon for me, with a .410 we kept near the back door. I collected six dollars for my "white dove" mount, which was about as much as hired help then earned for a day's work at harvest time. I soon had a collection of birds flying or standing around the room I shared with my brother, including a mallard and a blue winged teal, also collected for me by my father. The birds shared space with model airplanes hanging from the ceiling or sitting on the desk or chest of drawers. The models are long gone, but I have the mallard and the teal still.

My parents were occupied with dry-land farming and cattle husbandry, and the countless concerns weather, crops, cattle, and family demanded, but, like country folk everywhere, they never lacked interest in what we as family did, nor were they ever detached from their community; and their lives were rich with the interactions of neighbors, relatives, church, and all of the country business and social activities, from 4-H to farm sales. Some of the neighbors were relatives too. We traded labor with neighbors and relatives during harvest times, and no neighbor with a health problem or family crisis had to worry about what would happen to his cattle or crops if he or his family could not handle the situation. We harvested a neighbor's entire wheat crop for him one year when he was incapacitated, and that was a time before combines when we had to bundle, stack, and thresh everything. Before combines came, shelling and threshing were community activities, the women and girls getting together to prepare the huge noon "dinner" for the boys and men, who came in covered with dust and chaff and grease to wash, compare notes, and tell jokes. (*Com'on boys; after we wash up we can go to town and maybe get a little fresh stuff.* His wife behind him, *If you had a little more, you could get a little fresh stuff right here at home.*) In hot weather there might be a beer, but it would usually be delivered to the crew at the job site. "Lunch" did not exist in our world then: we ate breakfast, dinner, and supper, in that order.

My parents never said much about my activities outdoors or indoors so long as the chores or work got done, and I cannot remember ever being rebuffed or discouraged, whether my immediate interest was books, birds, taxidermy, music, photography, fishing, hunting, football, basketball, building something, or, later, girls. At the same time, they never indicated any expectation that I would spend my life with cattle or crops. I knew from a very early age that I was expected to go to college and become someone less dependent upon the vagaries of weather and markets, someone not always subject to hard and usually dirty, not to mention occasionally dangerous, physical labor. Even when I began building an airplane in the basement they did not question the project. Perhaps because I had built many models they assumed it was just another similar project on a bigger scale.

I remember buying some basic tools when my father and I were in the hardware store in Sarben, a tiny town near the "North River" that has long since ceased to exist. Some of the tools were useful for my taxidermy and some were for the new project. We had a whole shop full of tools, but my father apparently saw nothing wrong with my having some of my own. Actually, I needed the small vise I bought for the taxidermy shop I had set up in the basement, as the big vise in the big shop in the garage was the wrong size in the wrong place. It is a tool I have still, as is the leather-handled hammer I bought at the same time, tools that connect me to times and places, and are talismans almost as important to me as the memory of the sound of duck wings, my mother's singing in the kitchen, or my father's playing his harmonica, or swearing at a recalcitrant animal or skinned knuckle in two languages.

My Uncle Andy and Aunt Lydia and daughters lived in a big house in Sarben, and I had helped him with harvest. Probably that's were I got the money to buy the tools. I bought some light strips of molding from Kildare's Lumber Yard in Paxton to form the fuselage of my airplane. That was one project that did not get beyond the starting phase, but I never heard any criticism or discouraging questions. I suppose they knew that I was about to graduate from our one-and-a-half room country school (you had to take a test to graduate from the eighth grade in those days) and go to high school in town, which I did when I was thirteen, and the airplane project would come to a natural demise. I had created the outline of a P-40 before I abandoned construction. It was just big enough to sit in, but my experience with building flying models had already taught me that it would have been too heavy to fly anyway. Besides, I had run out of money.

I did have my first airplane ride soon after the war ended, when a neighbor, who learned to fly at age 65, took me up over the big lake (McConaughy) in his new Cessna 120. One of his sons had been a pilot in the war, and soon the entire family was flying. The view from above was wonderfully revealing, but I still remember how noisy that small airplane was and how surprised I was by the way he landed it in a series of stalls over the cottonwood trees and hanger to get it down on to the pasture strip. My father offered to finance flying lessons, but by that time I knew I was soon going out of state to college, and with a first son's sense of responsibility, did not think we should spend the money. Chances are, that was not only false economy, but selfish to boot. My father almost certainly would have enjoyed seeing me do it, but that would not have been something I was aware of then. It takes a while to learn that there are different kinds of selfish. There are lots of things I wish could "do over," as we would have put it then.

My interest in birds had begun when I was very young: I can't remember now whether the birds came first or the *Western Bird Guide—Birds of the Rockies and West to the Pacific*, already a classic I suppose, published in 1913, and given to me by a family friend who celebrated her birthday the same day I did, although she was sixty years older. It came from a library that must have been unique in the farm homes of the time, the home of the farming partner or associate of Grandpa

Mike, my mother's father. Mr. Lute, as he was always referred to, wrote occasional articles for the *Nebraska Farmer*. I do not know the exact business arrangement between that grandfather and Mr. Lute, but they lived in large homes as close as if they had been on large city lots, on the same farm in the North Valley. I know that my grandfather had the cattle. I remember the Lute library as having many high shelves filled with books, a gun cabinet with many guns, and especially a dried cotton plant complete with cotton bolls, a wonderfully exotic item that even as a child I recognized as from a far-away place. That library, with its books and guns and cotton boll, has to this day remained to my mind the metaphor for the good and complete life. I still have the bird guide, of course.

The interest in taxidermy, which was directly connected to my interest in birds, was inspired by the collection of ducks, geese, and other game birds and animals in Ole's Bar in town, where occurred my first realization that entire assortments of beautiful creatures could be possessed permanently. There had been a "stuffed" great-horned owl somewhere in the family too. I had admired especially the large, yellow, glass eyes. But it was Ole's displays, along with the walls covered with photographs of his hunting trips, that provided true inspiration: it was obviously possible to have such things as a row of live-looking waterfowl of all species on a shelf. Some could be made to look as if still flying, and attached to a wall. Ole is gone but his bar remains as "Ole's Big Game Bar." It is under different ownership now, but the birds are still there, at least they were there when I was back a few years ago, along with Ole's collection of animals from all over the world, including an upright polar bear in a glass case that looks down on you as you enter. You can get a meal there with your beer now and play Nebraska style keno too, or you can buy a hunting or fishing license. During the high school years, Ole sometimes took a few of us to school events in his Buick convertible. He always had a revolver strapped to his steering column in a holster made for that purpose. I assume it was protection for the roll of bills he always seemed to have. Given his occupation and his past as a minor league pitcher he may have been the only member of the community able to carry a big roll of bills—next to the banker anyway.

I saw the animals and photographs in Ole's only because my father would occasionally take me in when he went in to play the punch boards. For a nickel, dime, or quarter you could punch a folded piece of paper out of the board to see if you had won something. You might win money or candy, and I remember my father sometimes winning walnut rolls or almond bars. This was when I was very young, when we lived on the first and second farms near Paxton. Grandpa Fred, my father's father, was a punch board regular and was well known for winning boxes of cherry chocolates. My father never drank in the bar, indeed almost never drank at all. We would have wine at Thanksgiving and Christmas, and he would have a beer at harvest time. He kept whiskey in the house for medicinal purposes, but I never saw him drink any. He would mix a warm whiskey concoction when he had a bad cold, lift it to his lips as if to drink, and pour it down the sink. The story was that in his younger days, when he was "running the country" with Siff (my Uncle Andy) and Rip (my Uncle Roger)—father was "Tore"—they got some bad bootleg whiskey which made them so ill they thought they would die; and that experience provided a perfect cure. Apparently the contraband did not come from the family supply: another story had to do with how Grandpa Fred and family dismantled the still when the revenuers showed up in the farm yard.

PHS

No school buses came our way when we lived on the South Side, eight and a half miles from town. When I started Paxon High School, located on the second floor of an old, big, square, red brick building that housed all the grades, K-12, and had the gym in the basement, my father found a '37 Ford coupe with a rebuilt Mercury engine for my high school transportation. Learning to drive was not a concern as, like most farm and ranch boys, I had been driving something or other before I could reach the peddles without "scrouching" down, as we described it. In those days a country boy went to the court house and took a test and got a license to drive to school. I was thirteen when I got my driver's license. Of course it was restricted to driving to school, or school events. The "or school events" restriction meant I never missed anything I didn't want to miss. My father would crawl under the coupe about every other morning—no matter the weather—to adjust the mechanical brakes, which even during the best of times were a kind of delayed action apparatus. The brakes were such a delayed action device that I once crossed the busy Lincoln Highway, which I had to cross twice every day going to and coming from high school, without being able to stop. I could easily have been hit by one of the many trucks that used the highway. Coming up to the highway stop sign was always something of a thrill, even though I was careful every time. Another time the brakes delayed as I was turning to park at the bank. I almost hit my young, female math teacher, who was being cute, standing in the parking space and waving. She thought I was being fresh and jumped out of the way. I don't think she ever knew that I simply couldn't stop.

Dad never complained about fixing the brakes or coming to get me on the occasions when the Ford's radiator boiled over or the carburetor got plugged, rather regular occurrences, or gave me driving advice or questioned my activities, even after he and my mother attended the ball games when I started to play. The farm-ranch operation we ran was a family affair: boys were expected to be responsible and act as adults, and most of us did, most of the time. Indeed, when we country boys turned sixteen and were completely street legal, we usually drove our own vehicles to the out-of-town games. This saved space on the school bus for cheerleaders and other students. We drove ourselves to most activities. My parents would take short vacations and trips and leave the entire operation to me when I was fourteen. One of the things we learned growing up raising cattle and wheat on the shortgrass prairie was responsibility. It was real responsibility, not some invented importance. By that time the '37 coupe had been traded for a '47 Chevy convertible, tan with red trimmed seats and an under-the-seat heater that worked wonderfully during the cold school months when I drove to town listening to Fred Waring's Pennsylvanians on the car radio. I think that was the group, but in fact, I'm not absolutely sure. I would ask my mother if I could, for she remembered all such things. I think she could also remember every meal she had ever made and a good many cooked by someone else. She could probably confirm that my other favorite music program was the Sunday night Telephone Hour. I used to lie across a couple of our leather seated dining room chairs with my eyes closed and listen to it. Mother is gone now, of course, along with nearly everyone else who was so important to me in my growing and forever after. It is really their story I want to tell, but I don't know how to tell it except through myself; and I don't know how I could have told it before now. It was they who made our part of the vast semi-arid desert home.

During my daily drives to high school I had learned to be careful not only of the hills on the narrow, graveled roads, but also of the scent of the milking barn on my hands and the odor of corral on my shoes when I got to there. On special occasions I was allowed the new Chrysler New Yorker and one day was delighted to discover that its hood was longer than that of the Cadillac driven by a female classmate, who lived on a farm south of us. She was a very sensible country girl and good friend, who would sometimes fly over me when I was on a tractor doing field work and wiggle the wings of the family Cessna. I would tease her about needing so much sky to set up her landing. Later, when I was in college, and after that the Navy, and was home for vacation or on leave, we would drive the forty miles to North Platte for a movie. By then I got home only rarely, and she went off to college to become a lab technician. Things may have progressed farther, but one night while taking her home I ran over a skunk, and the car stunk so badly she went in and I went home. I was perhaps too philosophical about it, having learned at an early age how little things could foul big things up, so to speak. I had to leave again the next day anyway, but later I came to regret the skunk and heard in a round-about way that in other ways too I should have been paying more attention. Things never progressed to the point where my mother would have pointed out that she was Catholic and I was, at least nominally, Lutheran. Perhaps, even my mother would have remained silent, for by then my indifference to religion of any stamp must have been painfully obvious.

I don't remember the numbers of my freshman, sophomore, or junior years at PHS, but our senior class was twelve, six male, six female. I had known some of my classmates from kindergarten. From kindergarten through part of the third grade I had attended school in the same building before we moved to a different farm in a different county. Farm moves were always in March, which meant starting school in a different place toward the end of the school year. Though this happened three times, I cannot remember its being a hardship. One of the reasons that my memories of home move to different places and differing times is that home was first in the Paxton irrigated north valley, then in the Sutherland countryside, also irrigated, then back to the Paxton south side, meaning the dry land farming wheat country. None of these places was as much as thirty miles from the other, though, so home is really an amalgam, and because I always had relatives in all those places, the central social core was always stable.

High school was important, even though I always knew that it was, for me at least, not the end of formal education. There were students there I had known most of my life, activities that took us around the state, books, and teachers, most of whom one could respect. Singing with a group was possible; we had a debating group and some journalism, though most of journalism meant doing a yearbook. Classes were limited; there was nothing like a band, and football was of the six-man variety. If one wanted to take algebra beyond the first year, he had to do it by correspondence. Plane geometry was offered, but nothing beyond. We had one, memorable, at least to me, outstanding teacher who taught history and civics, Mr. Walter Murrish, an articulate and knowledgeable man, whose invariable shiny shoes got him his nickname. He began our debating group, and, naturally, after a couple of years moved on to a collegiate environment. Miss Lute, daughter of my paternal grandfather's long ago farming partner, taught English and Latin until my senior year. She was also knowledgeable, competent, and important to me. Mr. Mullins, our superintendent, was usually called "Moon." Yet, from my little graduating class of a dozen came three educators, two on the collegiate level, a medical technician, and a dentist, so my high school's limitations cannot be considered much of a handicap. Of the six boys in the class only one did not go on to college, and he had a prosperous wheat and cattle operation to go home to. Three or four of the boys did military service. Of the six girls, one went on and five married, soon after, or not very long after, graduation.

During the first years, school "got out" for Farm Day, a promotion by the John Deere company that included demonstrations, informative, entertaining, and instructional movies at the local theater, all demonstrating new farming methods using John Deere equipment. Food was provided. Our parents would be there too. It was a strange and wonderful day. Those of us from the country went to farm days, but I never thought to ask what the town kids did. A couple of my best friends lived in town. I traded nights at our houses with one of them, and can remember being highly amused once when he came out to spend the night in the country and had to bundle up completely to watch me load cane for the cattle, which I did bareheaded and barehanded. I remember thinking how it was that we got used to things physical and how we noticed the panting of the city folk carrying in new furniture, an activity that would not have caused any of us an extra breath.

One of the most important things about high school, simply put, was girls, some of whom seemed especially lovely then to a very young man with at least the normal ridiculous excess of male hormone, and who for a time tended to place the creatures on something of a pedestal. In those days they looked especially fetching in their fuzzy sweaters, bobby socks, saddle shoes, and long skirts, the skirts sometimes demurely hiked up a few inches and pinned with a little decoration in the form of a poodle or some other cute feminine figurine. "Going steady" was the respectable way to go about dating then, if you were serious about dating, and seemed to happen automatically if you took a girl to two movies. That's how I found out I was going steady. I found out that I was no longer going steady when I showed up at the third movie with my parents. The young lady immediately began going steady with someone else.

Besides the classes and home rooms, there were many places for opposite sexes to mingle: games, dances, school carnivals to make money, play and music rehearsals, interscholastic music and academic contests held out of town. The school dances happened frequently, it seemed to me, always in the gym and included some eighth graders too. I enjoyed them, for as school activities they gave me an excuse to drive to town legally. If you wanted to take a girl home, you learned to ask early. I was never very good at small talk, but managed somehow. As it turned out I usually danced most dances with Maxine, who was older than I was, but seemed to be one of the few girls who actually heard and moved to the music. Learning that the ability of girls to dance to the music was hardly universal was one of those small discoveries one makes with memorable surprise. It continued to be a surprise, even after I knew it. What on earth do they hear? I don't know when I first thought the world a rational place: girls are graceful creatures; therefore they should be able to hear and keep up with the beat, for example; but I have never been able to get over the thought, even now, knowing better. Winter meant getting together to go ice skating on the frozen sandpit near the north river. We brought discarded tires and burned them on the ice, and sometimes helped each other get our cars unstuck so that we could get back on the road. There were local celebrations, like Founders' Day, county fairs, and public dances. And there was always church.

Having always thought going steady stupid for persons of my age, (a thought my parents heartily subscribed to), and wanting to take more than one of the ladies to the movies or special affairs such as the junior-senior prom, I managed to date most of those I was interested in before, after, or between their more permanent attachments. Dating didn't automatically mean sex then, for in those days sex meant pregnant and pregnant meant marriage and marriage meant no college. Abortions were unheard of, and condoms were something you saw in dispensers in truck-stop restrooms. There was nothing strange or exotic about sex to a country boy who grew up seeing mares taken to stud, or could see it anytime by looking into the bull pasture (I wondered if any town kids had ever seen a bull masturbate), barn, or chicken house—or whose youngest brother was thirteen years younger. To watch the males in pursuit of the prettiest females always seemed too much like a pack of dogs pursuing a bitch in heat then too—obvious and about as disgusting as being asked once, while only a twelve-year-old waiting to be picked up by my parents in front of Bower's drug store, *Where can a guy get a piece of ass in this town anyway?* I assumed the question came from someone's hired men and would have been more shocked had I not been used to hired men, some of whom were habitually profane.

But one learned that the ladies could be good friends, smart and conversational—and after all, a little "petting" was permissible, and not permanently damaging. I did end up with a hat pin stuck through the top of my convertible one morning, the young lady apparently discovering she had no real need of it, probably to her disappointment—I don't really know, of course. I did let her know that holes in the canvas tops of convertibles were not a way to a man's heart, and remember the note she signed in my "Tiger," (our yearbook) stating that she had given up hat pins. It didn't matter, as her signing the yearbook was the last I ever saw of her. She was smart and personable, and I wished her well. I wish them all well, for the girls of PHS gave me, with the exchange of little gifts at Christmas, with their almost invariable good humor, with their matter-of-fact competence—and with their vulnerability—a confirmation of the human touch implicit in family. I didn't hang around town long enough to discover if one them might have shared a dark, starlit sky with mallards overhead. Perhaps I should have.

The incident reminds me, though, that under my senior picture in "Tiger," where some editor had made a descriptive statement, as he or she did for every member of the graduating class—something like, "She's one of music and talent," or "He's as pleasant as he is athletic," or such—mine read something like,

"Attention ladies; he's one in a million." I had no idea what that meant then and have no idea what it means now. Probably, whoever wrote it just needed something to write. I had probably missed any number of important things my senior year, since for me that year was only seven months long. I had learned enough of the ladies by then to know that if they were interested they had ways of letting you know—also the contrary, and could carry grudges and personal assessments rather farther than necessary, or so it seemed to me. In the four years high school took the early pedestal for girls evaporated too, not as epiphany, but in a series of small events like the unforgettable odor of a female friend standing near my home room desk as she said good morning, apparently in need of a bit more menstrual-time advice, and the extraordinarily lovely creature encountered in the big town (North Platte) who suddenly turned to spit in the street. Besides, I had already discovered the problem with dancing to the music. This was long before I learned that they had other idiosyncrasies too, like always opening boxes on the wrong end.

None of my class "got in trouble," as euphemism had it in the good ol' days; but my old friend from the country, Sam, managed to "knock up" his girlfriend, Jane; and though they seemed a perfect match and had been going together for a long time, they went their separate ways. And it's not that we lived in some kind of age of innocence: we knew about the farm wife who got bored enough with country life and her husband to bounce around on a pool table with a bartender in town, and about the northsider who went wild after her husband drowned when his tractor slipped into the irrigation canal, and I'm sure the men involved were known to someone too. Everyone knew of the local businessman who had a mistress. But somehow, testosterone rampant, autos handy, fuzzy sweaters prominent, we made it through. We were helped, perhaps, by the absence of television and a time when movies were mostly musicals with heroes like Howard Keel and Joel McCrea and heroines like Katherine Grayson, and westerns in which Roy Rogers followed Gene Autry who followed Hop-a-long Cassidy—and by a sense of family that demanded attention to certain principles in the relationships between sexes, especially if one was Lutheran and the other Catholic. No one will ever convince me that anyone other than one who had been a teenage boy could possibly understand the weight of hormones, their utter reliability and sheer inconvenience; or worse, their longevity.

Town and Country

Paxton, a town of fewer than 600 residents, is located in the valley of the South Platte on the Lincoln Highway and the Union Pacific railroad, not far from the river. When I was in high school it had a grocery store and two saloons and a number of small businesses catering to farming and ranching. There was a bank and a drugstore and a Plymouth-Chrysler dealership. You could buy an Oliver tractor or machinery made by International Harvester. When I was a child it had a blacksmith shop, a dentist, and a doctor, but they were long gone when I went to high school. The nearest medical facilities of any kind were twelve miles away from Paxton, and we lived eight and a half miles from town. I understand the town was named for a railroad official, and in the early days had been called Alkali. On the north edge of town the range of sandhills that ran between the two Plattes began. You crossed from one valley to the other through Windy Gap. Just before you got to Windy Gap you saw the water tower for the town with the big "Paxton" on it. Only main street was paved. If you went there today you would find not only Ole's Big Game Bar functioning still, but the store and bank—and the water tower. The bankers owned the farm we lived on then.

The word was that my father had proposed to my mother at Windy Gap. The pass was steep and sandy, and my uncles said they sometimes had to back a Model-T over the pass to gravity feed fuel from a less than full tank to the engine. Less than full tanks were common then as money was scarce, even for twenty-cents-a-gallon gasoline, or maybe it was ten cents during the time my uncles were remembering, as history says it was when I was born. Money was always scarce and a major topic of conversation.

The farm then, with enough pasture to help support our cattle operation, was the fourth and last of the farms my family lived on, a section and a half, almost a thousand acres; and like the others we rented it. We were "southsiders," living south of the South Platte, where dry-framing was practiced, as opposed to "northsiders," who lived in the broad North Platte valley and enjoyed the advantages of irrigation furnished by the Platte Valley Project—"The Project." The "sandhillers," lived in the grasslands north of the farm country. For some reason my father referred to the sandhillers as "wrinkle bellies." I can only speculate why. Unlike most of our neighbors, who owned most of, or at least much of, the land they farmed or ranched, we were always renters. My father never seemed much concerned that he did not own the land he lived on: perhaps it was because there was land in the family. The sandhill pasture we ran our Herefords on in summer belonged to his mother (his father was dead by then), and he paid his mother rent, which was part of her income. She also owned wheat land in the "south country"; "Spoolerville" it was called. From her properties she received enough income to die at ninety-three a wealthy lady. The Spoolerville land was sometime called "The Homestead," but I do not know whether that title referred to a place of beginning or a homestead in the legal sense, for my grandparents got to America from Russia in the 1890's, and I know they had been involved in many other activities before coming to their semi-desert home. I learned that they lived on the homestead in a basement house for a time. A basement house is a house consisting of a basement only, until enough time and money permitted adding the house itself. Basement houses were quite common when I was growing up: several of my relatives and a neighbor lived in them. They were very efficient, warm in winter and cool in summer, and still in use when I went to high school. My paternal grandparents did not live on the homestead when I was born, although they always owned it, but on rented land in the north valley, where the land could be irrigated, and the crops were not limited to corn and wheat, but could include sugar beets, potatoes, and alfalfa. I never saw the homestead.

Why buying land had not the same huge priority evinced by the neighbors I do not know. My parents always had enough to provide for education, never encouraging any of us to stay on the farm: my two brothers and I went to college out of state. My sister attended college briefly in state before attending a vocational business school and marrying. One brother, after a stint in the Navy, became a petroleum engineer; and "little" brother, after a tour flying helicopters in Viet Nam became a veterinarian. Perhaps farming and ranching were considered too hard and too uncertain. Certainly, all our early years were filled with worries—worries about the weather, worries about the crops, worries about the animals, especially worries about the vagaries of the weather. We once calculated that seven things could destroy a wheat crop: too little rain, too much, black rust, red rust, hail, too much wind, insects. Everything from lightning and coyotes to bovine disease could kill cattle. Income was always uncertain and always variable. But there were good years, when the crops were abundant and the cattle were valuable enough to have afforded their buying their own place. They talked about it occasionally and knew the details of ownership in a large area, and I remember one trip actually to look at a stock farm in another county. It looked good to a boy: it had a creek and trees—something exceptional in our country; but I can remember a remark about its being marginally productive. When my father died there was enough money from the sale of cattle, wheat, granaries, machinery, and the other ten thousand things used in a cattle and wheat operation to provide my mother a nearly new house in town, income to live comfortably for twenty years, and funds to help family members in their living and setting up careers. No one in my immediate family was ever without a place to go for help.

Though my father's parents lived in the north valley then, they had once had a farm in Wyoming but were "dried out," as they put. We had visited the Wyoming place a time or two, and even as a child I found their farm there unappealing. What I remember most are long, dusty, treeless, roads and empty fields.

I never really liked Grandpa Fred. I'm sure as a child I was afraid of him. I don't know whether the disliking was instinctive or began because he had large, fierce, growling dogs that always ran out in rather savage greeting when we came to visit, and were extremely frightening to a child. He was actually never unkind to me, giving me an occasional dime and once a wagon for Christmas, and there was always a bag of Christmas candy; but our grandparents then were not the doting kind, even though I was the first grandchild in a very large family. As I got older I was able to justify my dislike through the family history I learned.

Grandpa Fred was a big man, well over six feet tall, at least 250 pounds, with a thick gray, wiry shock of hair and a large iron-gray mustache. He was brusque and very strong, able to throw a hundred pound sack of "spuds" from the ground into a truck. He smelled of cigars and had to have his daily Schnapps. His five sons always referred to him as "The Old Man," but it was a descriptive phrase; there was never a tone of disrespect; it was simply given as a statement of fact.

Grandpa Fred had been orphaned, had deserted the Russian army, into which he had been conscripted, had thrown away his rifle and swum the Nieper River to escape eventually to Germany. He had been fired upon in his attempt and nearly drowned when the heavy woolen cape, fastened with a chain around his neck, had become waterlogged. He had been able to tear it away. He was one of many of German ancestry whose forebears had gone to Russia at the invitation of Katherine the Great and who left when conscription began, although they had been in Russia 150 years. In Russia they had been orchardists and carpenters and I'm sure other things I never heard about. There was the usual joke about their having been horse thieves. They insisted they never fraternized with the "Goddamnbulchiviks," which was one word in Grandpa Fred's vocabulary, but when I had daughters of my own I insisted there must have been a Mongol in the fagots somewhere to explain my daughters' beautiful almond-shaped eyes. There was a story that all our relatives in the Ukraine had been speared as they hid in haystacks. I have no idea whether this was true. We received Russian candies and painted wooden spoons from relatives in Lincoln or Omaha at Christmas time, but whether there was a direct Russian connection I never knew. The anti-military sentiment was a constant in the family until three of Grandpa Fred's five sons had to go to war during WWII. Until that time nothing positive was heard about anything military in my family. In Germany, as the story continued, he had worked for an abusive farmer. He got even by tying the sheeps' mouths with white thread so they starved. Somehow he had worked his way to the United States. If he had help from relatives, I never heard about it.

Perhaps, it was the small scar on my father's forehead and the tales that followed that over the years justified my distaste, or at least indifference to Grandpa Fred. The scar was the result of being struck by a tug, a heavy, leather, harness part, when my father attempted to protect his mother, Grandma Katherine to us, from spousal abuse. In another incident my father was knocked down a set of stairs—same offence. Later, a thyroid problem—goiter in those days—was discovered and given the blame. Another occasion, when my father himself had become a married man living on the "First Farm," was the discovery of his father stealing his irrigation water, as they had adjoining fields. Because the water was rationed by the "ditch company" and you had only the days to water apportioned to you, my father threatened to kill him with the shovel in hand, an incident that garnered permanent respect and another family story about how one secured his place in the universe. I never learned if that was before or after the "goiter operation."

When he was 65, Grandpa Fred broke his leg and gangrene set in. He refused to allow the amputation, the only solution, with a *Goddamnit, I came into this world with two legs, and I'm going out with two.* He died in terrible agony on a Christmas Day. But he had lived the American dream, coming to the country without any help that we had ever heard of and dying a prosperous owner of property and cattle. His days had come to include a daily cigar with his Schnapps, and his years included new GMC trucks. He was unusually successful at selling his potato crop and had a wide acquaintanceship, all of whom must have shown up at his huge funeral—the size of the funeral there and then always a sign of success.

Grandma Katherine, whose spoken English was sufficient, but always heavily accented, managed a household of five sons, four daughters, and a daughter of a daughter, who was treated as a daughter and whose antecedents were never spoken of. I was taught to speak of her as an aunt. Grandma's reading was limited to her German Bible. In later years, when she lived alone in her house in town with

Uncle Fred, she became an addict of TV soaps, and with those, her garden, occasional church, and visits from and ever-increasing circle of relatives lived out her days in a town of under 600 which was residence to 60 widows. Uncle Fred and Uncle John farmed together and cared for Grandma Katherine's interests, but never managed land of their own. Grandma Katherine could have helped all her offspring to farms or businesses, but, either fearfully or selfishly, or maybe wisely, she kept what she had to herself and dying intestate left the business of dividing her estate to state law, in so doing helping lawyers and distant family "relations" as far away as Greece instead. It probably did not matter much, for by then the offspring were all in their 60's and 70's and most had earned their way far from the land. But in my family one did compare, for my mother's side approached life somewhat differently.

Before moving to the country my father's family had been located in Lincoln, from where in summer the large family migrated to beet fields for work, as far away as Montana. In winter Grandpa Fred had a coal hauling business in those early years, and relating that time always included the comment that his business partner was black. Their neighbors across the road from the north valley place were Japanese, and by then sugar beets were worked by Mexican families from Mexico by way of Texas. The family my grandfather hired year after year was headed by Joe Gonzales, "Little Joe," as the neighborhood knew him. Little Joe had twenty-five living children and lived in a small, unpainted but tight "beet house" not far from the main farm yard. He was a small man but a prodigious, responsible worker. A contemporary of Little Joe's was once heard to remark, *Leetle Joe, he fuckay too much; he have too much keeds.* When we lived on the second farm, I rode to school with some of Little Joe's kids, and though their noses sometimes ran and they smelled of garlic, they were clean and bright and very artistic, and beyond that I didn't think about it. Later, at our third farm, when we had a Mexican family of our own, the boys and I played cowboys and Indians together; their sisters, whom I thought beautiful, sometimes helped out in the house; and my father taught the men to handle machinery and irrigate after the beet work was done. My parents were invited to attend the Mexican weddings and came back home with delighted descriptions of the ceremonies and food.

We saw Grandpa Fred and Grandma Katherine frequently while they were on their north valley farm. Sometimes our earlier visits included dinner and sometimes dinner included a carp, a fish not generally though highly of in our country; but my grandmother would prepare one or two a year. They seemed perfectly edible to me.

Their house had numbers of special dishes behind a large cabinet with a thick door of curved glass. Some of the dishes were made of painted wood, and there were spoons too of painted wood. The dinner table was huge, with large round legs of oak. The kitchen was a metal arrangement, white metal sink, white, metal cabinets, white everything. Once, when I was very small, I remember uncle Hank building a wooden boat in the dining room. He was putting it together with brass screws. Uncle Hank loved duck hunting and raising American water spaniels, which he would show off by putting his glove on top of a fence post and having a dog jump to retrieve it.

Outside Grandpa Fred and Grandma Katherine's house was a windmill with wooden vanes. They were white too, like the kitchen. Nearby was the "spud cave," a long trench in the ground with a roof on it big enough to back a truck into. It was always cool and damp and always smelled of potatoes, though you might find other things there too, like watermelons and onions and big crocks of sour kraut and pickles.

When we got older, we took shotguns or rifles with us on some of our visits to our north valley grandparents. Doves and pheasants were abundant during the hunting seasons. If bird hunting was slow we could take pot shots at the prairie dogs that lived in the prairie dog town between the main house and the little house my Uncle Harry and Aunt Elma lived in after he got back from places like Guadalcanal, or we could listen to the talk about crops and cattle or about the old days. Uncle Harry had been an amphibious vehicle driver in the South Pacific during the big war and didn't ever say much except that sometimes the bilge pumps pumped blood. Aunt Elma had at one time been one of our hired girls. Uncle Harry tried farming for awhile after he got home from the Army, but he never really prospered at it and ended up working for the ditch company.

The mourning doves would usually be among the trees along the large irrigation canal just north of the house. The fields, corn, alfalfa, potatoes, small grain, stretched to the north, below the ditch. That's where the pheasants usually were. You got to the fields over a wooden bridge built of heavy planks which made a big clunking sound when you drove over it. I sounded sometimes as if you were "rolling it up." Beyond the fields was the main valley road; divided from the road by a narrow strip of meadow land was a railroad. Then came the trees along the North Platte, after the dams were in place and let the trees grow, where red-headed woodpeckers and bobwhite quail liked to hang out, and finally came the Sandhills proper, so still and stolid. You could see all of this from the ditch bank, as it was higher than the fields below. It was to me always an impressive panorama: fields, trees, hills; and you could see not only across the valley but also east and especially west a very long way. In fall and winter when we went to the river for pheasants or ducks or quail, huge flocks of prairie chickens and sharptail grouse would fly over us to the fields to forage or sit awkwardly on haystacks. They migrated from the Sandhills to the valley every winter. The hunting season was closed for them then, but the sight of their huge flocks flying over with those special cupped wings is unforgettable. With their cupped wings and flying in flocks, they were a lot like flights of mallards.

Except for the presence of the railroad, you would have thought yourself in an isolated valley, quiet, contained, unchangeable. Trains were infrequent then, but when I was very young I could still take the train west from Sarben to see my Bayard grandmother. Everyone called the train the "Toonerville Trolley." It hasn't carried passengers for a very long time but is busier than ever now carrying Wyoming coal to huge power generating plants in Nebraska and Missouri and elsewhere. One of the power plants is located on the Sutherland Reservoir and keeps the water warm enough that waterfowl can winter there. I think the railroad is part of the Burlington-Northern system. I took it several times, riding alone to see Grandma Molly and her second husband for a week and get treated to 7-up and comic books, new acquaintances and small town life; and I always had the time to build another model airplane. The main valley road went east past Sarben, the only reminder of its former days then a large, free-standing concrete vault that had been part of the bank, and then on to Sutherland and North Platte. To go west you had to first go north, then cross the North Platte River bridge, and turn west on a sandy track through the twenty-one section Sieleson Ranch. If you stuck to it, you could eventually end up north of Ogallala. At one time, the Lute family, who had farmed with my maternal grandfather, owned all the land south of the river from Sarben west to far beyond the bridge. They still owned a farm nearly across the road from Grandpa Fred and Grandma Katherine. For a long time, my uncles Fred and John farmed it. I was able to hunt it then for mallards, pheasants, and quail. That was after Uncle Fred returned from his service in Panama during the big war.

Uncle Fred never married. The story was that he had been madly in love with Mother's sister Esther, and could see no one else ever; so when she turned him down he gave the whole business up. Uncle John married into the family of Grandpa Mike's brother, meaning he also had a wife of the same last name, just as my father had, so there should have been no problem with having children; but Uncle John and Aunt Marie never had a child. The was a series of miscarriages. Both uncles were farmers all their lives, sometimes for others, sometimes for themselves, sometimes together.

The Egington Place and the Sandhills

If you were to fly over the southside wheat country you would see countless fields as squares and rectangles marked by barbed wire fences, with farmsteads and their shelterbelts scattered randomly somewhere within the straight north-south, east-west lines and an occasional natural, empty-looking space that would be pasture. Most of the roads would be gravel, but there would be some pavement other than the main highways too. Nowadays you would also see countless perfect circles denoting "pivot" irrigation systems drawing water from the huge Ogallala Aquifer. The pivots were just beginning to spurt their circles on the prairie when I was there.

If you were to fly over the sandhills, however, you would be looking down an what appeared to be a gigantic ancient beach, with the waves perfectly delineated, all running in the same direction. For that's what the sandhills of Nebraska are, huge, sandy waves that through time were covered with short grass—a veritable sea of grass. In some of the troughs between the waves will be lakes, scores of lakes in some places; and other low places might be rich with cattails and tall grass as the water from the aquifer is at the surface. In the old days it was bison country. If you don't know your way around, you can still get lost. Except for main highways you would find no paved roads, few roads at all, in fact; but there will be sandy, two tracked trails. There will be cattle trails too, always ending at some windmill tank. You might remember that the sandhills have their own species of termite, living in the cow chips that have replaced the buffalo chips of the past. The lakes and marshes still there are home to waterfowl and fish.

When we ran our cattle there one of our wells had to be only sixty feet deep. That same well today goes down one hundred sixty feet, for the pivots sucking the Ogallala Aquifer in the south country—and now in the sandhills too—have been pumping water, water that took a million years to get there from the Rocky Mountain Front Range, much faster than it can be regenerated. Many sub-irrigated meadows have disappeared, some small lakes too; and some windmills are now without water. It's drier from Birdwood Creek to the Dismal River, country I know, and beyond, though water still flows in the Loups and the Niabrara.

Some of the big ranches are now owned by outsiders who come to raise bison and play cowboy and land their planes on paved strips once a year for the grouse season, for the greater prairie chicken and the sharptail grouse yet provide hunting of native birds found in old shooting prints. It's grand country for someone used to it, though the glorious, fiery sunsets mainly just predict another day of strong wind, just as they do in the south country. It's good cow country still, where you can run a hundred "pairs" on a section. A pair is a cow and a calf. Old traditions survive: if you help work the cattle, you will be invited to dinner; and dinner will be a banquet including steak, homemade bread, potatoes, corn, and homemade pie for dessert. There will probably be a place for the crew to "wash up" outside.

Our major operation on the fourth farm where the mallards flew was in wheat and cattle, always with a little or a lot of cane, though we had begun by raising corn also. My father was always among the first to try new strains of grain or methods of tillage. You could tell our pasturage at home and in the sandhills, thirty miles north, from adjacent pastures because our grass was thicker and higher than the grass across the fence. My father would never over-pasture as it was called, putting more animals in a area than was good for it. Most of his concern was practical: he wanted our animals to be in good condition, and he wanted a sustainable program, even in dry years; but part of his concern was esthetic. He liked rich pasture. He liked driving through it, and he liked walking over it, often picking up arrow heads from the sandhill "blowouts" and eventually had a beautiful collection of perfect points mounted and framed and hanging in the living room. He knew the grasses, that blue grama was the most nutritious, that the ancient buffalo grass had become sparse but was equally good and especially important in dry weather when it would bunch up and survive, that the tall and short sandgrasses held the sandy soil well. Why the yucca we called soapweed grew where it did we could never figure out. It grew abundantly in some places, not at all in others that looked identical.

When we first arrived on the dry-land farm we had to learn some new ways, as we had always had irrigated farms before. Summer tilling, as it was called, had not yet come into wide use. We planted the wheat between the corn rows with narrow drills made just for that purpose. That meant the land got no rest and the crops were not really very productive on our semi-desert area where rain averaged only about seventeen inches annually. My first tractor responsibility there was on the Farmal rowcrop tractor cultivating corn. We called it "laying by" the corn. Once, when a female cousin asked what I was doing, she was told that I was "laying by the corn." Her remark was, *That Dick, he always was kind of lazy.*

We planted pumpkins and squash between the corn rows, and we always planted about twenty rows of sweet corn, which matured much earlier than the field corn, a good thing at least for our purpose—summer consumption. I don't think we ever let any of the sweet corn mature for seed. Harvesting the pumpkins and squash was a delightful fall activity unlike the cold weather activity of har-

vesting the corn itself. My father soon changed the farming operation to summer
tilling, a regimen that left alternate fields fallow for a complete growing year,
though they were tilled to keep the weeds off. Weeds used moisture, and the idea
of summer tilling was to give a field two years' moisture, which produced far better yields. We stopped raising corn altogether, but we continued to raise some
cane or milo for livestock feed. Sometimes we raised oats. One of my most dis-
tasteful jobs was grinding oats for feed, for oat dust was a terrible irritant that
always seemed to go down my back. The only way to stop the itch was to take a
bath. It was good when we stopped grinding oats, instead taking them to an elevator to have them rolled in molasses as better baby beef feed in our 4-H projects.
We used rolled oats after we quit raising oats too, buying them instead. Not
grinding oats was one of the best advances in agriculture we ever made, so far as I
was concerned. In later years we had some alfalfa, mostly to hold soil, but it did
supply a small supplement to the hay we had to buy.

We eventually had a hay "sled" built, a huge platform on steel beams and tires
on which one could haul an entire haystack. We pulled the sled with a tractor to
the north valley, where we bought hay, sometimes from my uncles, unhitched the
tractor and pulled the haystack on to the sled with a cable. The sled bed tilted to
the side to let the stack slide on. Then we reattached the tractor and pulled the
whole thing home. The rig took nearly half the road. Getting a hay stack was
pretty much an all day job, but it did bring home a lot of hay. Eventually, however, after I was gone, of course, the sled was replaced by bales and machinery
that could handle them efficiently.

Hay sleds could be dangerous too. One rancher acquaintance, using horses
instead of a tractor, fell under the sled and the horses pulled it over him. Nails
protruding underneath cut him up. Accidents of all kinds were an unfortunate
part of farm-ranch living: Uncle Andy lost three fingers trying to clear an auger;
Uncle Hank was nearly killed when his sheepskin coat got caught in a power-
take-off; my father had his incidents with the Morgan and the Holstein; at various times I had a foot nearly crushed in a machine, was bitten and trampled by
horses and trampled by cattle; and one of our sandhill neighbors flew his Piper
into the ground while circling his ranch house. This is just a sampling which
doesn't even include most of the things that happened in my immediate family,
like a cut that had the blood spurting, or splinter that ran through a foot from
arch to instep.

The farm then represented endless work and responsibility for all of us, of
course, but it represented a good deal more too: it provides my spatial orientation
still. I merely have to imagine myself going up the long, sloping hill in the pasture

behind the house and facing south, where the house was, or north, toward the fences that bordered the road, over which was our north pasture; or I can imagine I face east to where the sun came up and where a mile and a-half away the Lehls lived, or west where the sun went down, and where we had a mile of tilled fields or crops, depending on the year, and where just out of sight was the Mennonite community—and I can sort out my directions. I can almost hear the wind and feel it on my face, for the hills always provided at least a breeze, and I see yet in memory with little effort the house itself, south from my orientation hill, stolid behind the shelterbelt we ourselves had planted.

Frequently then I ran the pastures on the home place to get or check on the cattle we kept at home. It took less time to run than to catch and saddle a horse, and I didn't have to bother with a gate. The horses were ridden enough to keep them manageable, but were kept mainly for use in the sandhills, or for herding the cattle north in spring and south in the fall. Sometimes we just took a car or pickup to check on pasture north of the house. But unless I took the .22, just in case I ran into a coyote, I ran.

I roamed the place, especially in spring and summer when the lagoons could contain water and wildlife: ducks nested some years, and the call of the killdeer was always nearby. In spring there might be phalaropes swimming in their perpetual little circles. Long-billed curlews often called from the pastures. The big lagoon near the house shelterbelt was near an active prairie dog town where in springtime the animals jumped and made their distinctive whistles and burrowing owls bowed from the mounds near the burrows, and from the fence posts. In spring the pheasants crowed from the fencerows and fields.

There were times when I lay on my stomach near the shelter belt and picked off a few prairie dogs with my .22, which I had scope sighted for that purpose. It was the only humane way we had to keep the town from taking up too much of the south pasture. The alternative was poison which we would not even consider. We liked the prairie dog town; we just had to keep it in check. Then, some years later, came an extremely unwise Nebraska law; and I got home from college one spring to find that the state had—by law—poisoned the entire town. One can be furious and sad at the same time. Later the state discovered how stupid the law was and recanted, but we never got our dog town back, or the same number of burrowing owls, extremely beneficial grasshopper eaters.

Summers were hot and sometimes we hated the wind, which could be incessant, but we knew it drew our water and, in the earlier years, made our electricity. Winters were unpredictable: some years December meant shirtsleeves, some years blizzards. We could have bad storms through April. One year the snow buried the chicken house and all the cattle feed. We couldn't get to or from town predictably for a month. But even in winter I roamed the hills and fields, sometimes on skis, sometimes on skis with my .22 rifle slung. I can't imagine how a boy could survive without all that space—without all that freedom and all that serious responsibility, or without a car and a .22 rifle.

Our south facing glassed-in porch was often warm enough to sit in, even in cold weather. It was a perfect place to read, sitting on the glider, or dream, or take a nap, or go through a Stoeger's catalog and look at the guns and wish for one that would take the kind of game one saw in Ole's Big Game Bar. The *National Geographics* were kept out there too. Eventually, I actually got a rifle pictured in the Stoeger catalog, the one I read about most. My father brought it home one day, having bought it from Ole himself. It was almost new. Dad took me deer hunting in Wyoming, a reward for staying out of school and drilling the wheat when he had surgery. I was sixteen then. I was not expecting a reward, but it was a boy's dream come true.

We rented a cabin near Woods Landing in Wyoming and hired a guide from the ranch that had the cabins. It was all very exotic, with dark roads between forests of scented pine trees, mountain peaks, and huge boulders, one of which I sat on to shoot a deer. On the way back Dad stopped in Cheyenne to buy a handsome, wool, western shirt, which hangs in my closet now as a memento.

Autumn could be the finest time of all, for if the lagoons were full there would be ducks and a chance to hunt. Once, while I lay on my stomach watching ducks come in to a big cornfield lagoon, a reddish roan coyote appeared, stalking carefully. Suddenly, to my complete puzzlement, he turned tail and ran. Almost immediately a large flock of ducks landed. Their whistling wings had frightened him off. He was obviously able to hear them long before I could and was either too inexperienced to know what the sound meant, or the sound meant some kind of danger he knew about, like a bullet coming his way. Fall meant the best weather of the year: it meant wheat drilling, and getting the cattle by horseback, out of the sandhills where they had spent the summer. It meant calf weaning time and days of loudly bawling animals and sorting cattle and trucking some to the sale barn in North Platte. Fall mean gathering the pumpkins and squash from between the corn rows, in the early days when we raised corn. Fall meant dove and prairie chicken season. It meant hunting for pheasants and ducks. Fall also meant football, but playing football didn't interfere with anything important somehow, and I didn't play my senior year anyway, suffering from a dust created cough and hoping to be better at basketball time.

Spring was too special to be involved in school sports. When the ducks returned to the lagoons in spring I had to be there to watch. I never went out for track. I had had enough of school by then anyway. Spring meant thirty miles on horseback herding the cattle to summer pasture in the sandhills. Spring meant early field work and crappies at Sutherland Reservoir or crappies or perch or white bass at Lake McConaughy or a trip to Wellfleet Lake or back to the sandhill lakes just to fish.

I knew and still know the location of every lagoon, every hill, every track, every fence line on the place; and I know my way into and out of the sandhills; I know the lakes and reservoirs, and both river valleys and all the towns along them from North Platte to Scottsbluff, and north to Valentine and south to Grant or McCook, the ragged and the level, the arid and the watered, the peopled and the empty—mostly empty. I know well this land that nurtured my people and nurtured me, the harsh, unpredictable, unforgiving, occasionally lovely, normally lonely, semi-desert, short grass or mixed grass prairie. Home—home, the place where you are not supposed to be able to go again, which is all right, for in the deepest, personal sense, though I have not lived there for a long time, I never left.

My father never complained or even commented about who he was or what he did. He had been born in Ohio and had come west with his family at a very tender age, spoke German before he knew English, went to school in Lincoln. He said the family came to Nebraska by wagon. I know nothing of the Ohio experience, except he said the town was Holgate, and now there is no one to ask about it. His English was totally without accent, but country grammar occasionally slipped out, even after he married my mother. To me he was a true cattleman and a genuine steward of the land. He hadn't finished eighth grade because he had to assume adult responsibilities in the operations of his large family, but he knew all the latest agricultural science from *Capper's Weekly* and *The Nebraska Farmer*. I can see him now, lying on his side after a long, cold day outdoors, propped up on one elbow, reading one of those publications in the red glow of the ceramic briquettes of our free-standing propane-fired furnace in the long farmhouse room that acted as a combination dining room and office. It was his pre-bedtime routine.

I can't remember ever hearing my father raise his voice in those years, except at animals, when he could be vociferous and profane, and swear in two languages. Those occasions were rare as he not only knew how to handle animals but had names for most of them, and he knew the history of every one, heifer, cow, bull, or steer. We had quarter horses, rather than work horses by this time, the last team, dapple grays Dutch and Esther, long since replaced by Olivers and International Harvesters and John Deeres. At one time my father had a racing quarter horse trained, but the horse was not a success. He was fast enough but never learned to leave the gate with the other horses. Thinking of my family or myself, he seems to fit right in.

Dad loved to fish and shoot an occasional bird, and he shot a deer near the South Platte River once. He had to have roses in the extensive garden he and my mother always seemed to have time and energy for, and when canning time came was an equal partner in the kitchen with my mother. He was very good with his hands, and in his younger days when corn was picked by hand was known to out-pick any other picker in the area, which was a good thing as pickers were paid by the bushel. But he could also fill a bucket with berries quicker than anyone else, or peel a peach. He had been a butcher in the early married years, cutting meat for a "fancy hotel in Lincoln," as he put it, had been a trapper, and was the neighborhood's unofficial veterinary at castrating time.

I can remember only one reprimand from this most important man in my growing up then, a very quiet, *Ah Dick*. I don't know that I could have worked for him in my mature years as we had the same kind of independent need of control, but I feel nothing but endless thankfulness for my good fortune in the way I grew up, part of an important, family enterprise full of mutual trust and respect and care and undemonstrative love. And undemonstrative it was: in later years when I came home to visit, we shook hands. Men did not hug in my family. You kissed your mother or grandmother on the cheek. You shook your uncles' hands, said *Hi*, to your aunts and cousins or shook hands.

I carry in my mind countless pictures of my father and events with my father, one of those persons I most miss—even now after all these years—in the every lengthening panoply of persons who have given my life meaning and dimension, and are gone forever. I see him as a young man, six feet and almost skinny from loading sugar beets by hand with a beet pitching fork, throwing forkful after forkful over his head on the truck, or slinging hundred pound bags (sacks we called them) on and off the truck, or unloading them in the shed of the potato chip maker in North Platte after making a deal at fifty cents a hundred, or a "buck," or in really good times, "two bucks." I see him in a woolen two-piece swimming suit dipping in the North Platte, a river too fast to swim in, too cold even in summer, and usually too shallow. I see him playing the harmonica, and have little trouble hearing *My Blue Heaven*, or *Molly and Me*, or *Red Sails in the Sunset*. I can picture him now in his Sunday best coming out of Bower's Drug Store after church with the usual Sunday quart of vanilla ice cream, a special extravagance. He was never anything but a totally decent man, to me, to anyone. I heard once that he could be mean, but I never saw it. During the early years at the Egington place my father still shaved with a straight razor, the razor strap hanging in the bathroom he added to the house. He would hang it on a chair to strop his razor. This was at a time in which discipline and the razor strap were part of conventional lore, but my father never once mentioned it, never threatened with it; I can't imagine he ever even thought of it in that way, and I certainly wouldn't even have known about its potential use myself except for boy talk and movies.

It would be hard to forget the time he first mounted a "newly broke" Morgan, a horse that squealed and pitched like a mad, wild mustang with no hint of the training he was supposed to have had. Not given to foolish heroics, my father jumped off and flattened to the ground just in time to avoid having his head kicked off. (This all happened on the Sutherland Place.) And it would be hard not to remember his encounter with a maddened Holstein on this, the Egington Place: I heard the bawling and crashing in the milking barn and rushed in to find the beast trampling him into the concrete gutter. One has all the strength one needs at such times: with a "beller" (bellow) of rage that must come from deep inside us from more primitive times, I took all eleven hundred pounds of crazed animal off my father with a tackle around her neck. He suffered four broken ribs and hurt for a long time.

In the middle and later years my father raised wheat in large fields where the soil was rich and black, and in strips where the soil was sandy and needed protection from the wind, which blew almost incessantly over the shortgrass plain that was our home. He liked to walk out into the waist-high stalks and check the heading grain and pull out the occasional clump of volunteer rye that grew there too.

One "fly in the ointment," to use the ordinary vernacular, was the interference of the federal government in our wheat operation. We didn't need the program and did not want to be involved in subsidies and stayed out of "the program" as long as we could. There came a time, however, when if you didn't "voluntarily" join you could not sell your wheat. Government agents actually came out and measured everyone's fields. *Damn good thing they don't have a "cattle program"* my father would say.

I know that one of his greatest joys was the cattle. Every week in summer meant a trip to the sandhills, in McPherson county, to check the windmills and tanks and look over the herd and take blocks of salt and minerals to replenish the wooden salt boxes near the windmill tanks. It was a sixty or seventy mile round trip. Sometimes more than one trip was necessary, with a mill to fix or a cow to treat for pink-eye or a new calf to vaccinate and brand. Before the pickup was four-wheel drive some of the trips were more like adventures with the narrow sandy tracks that acted as roads, for either the sand or, when it rained, the water could bog down a vehicle. We spent six hours once getting unstuck, finally using fence posts "borrowed" from a nearby fence to build a road under the tires. Another time we came out of the hills with a leather shoestring for a fan belt. Then there was the caretaker whose cows always had quintuplets while some of ours looked for their calves, lightning that destroyed twenty heifers in one stroke, and coyotes that would kill five newborns in a season. We raised purebred Herefords and owned one of the oldest brands in the state, and could put our "O-Bar" almost anywhere on the animal, though we invariably chose the left flank. In the later years, my father presented a trophy at the county fair to the 4-H stockman who won the best ribbon with one of his heifers, and he had the O-Bar brand painted on the doors of the pickup. In one of my favorite photographs Dad is standing near the pickup door with the brand on it, wearing his Stetson.

My father helped Uncle Hank get started in farming, providing him with haying equipment or the means to get it, and there was help in other ways, usually labor between the brothers, when there was hay to haul or crops to get in. Ironically, he had to ask Uncle Hank to leave the sandhill pasture once, when we caught him driving a group of Omaha "sports" through the tinder dry grass in search of prairie chickens. A hot muffler could have started a prairie fire that might have destroyed our entire summer range. Uncle Hank was indignant, but he left. Dad simply shook his head in wonder at his brother's lack of common sense.

It was a time when a man was expected to be aware of the dangers of prairie fires and the needs of cattle and crops when a man's word truly was his bond; at least that is the way my father lived. To him it was not a cliché. Of course, as in any time, some were not so honest. When the great war was going on new equipment was in short supply, a local dealer in machinery took advantage of the situation by demanding money "under the table" for the price-controlled machinery that came his way. My father had to pay an extra $1200 in cash in one instance to get the new corn-picker we had to have during those early corn years. There was too much corn to pick by hand, and getting dependable help during the war years was impossible. When the war ended, and equipment again became available, no farmer or rancher would have anything to do with the dealer. He had to go out of business, and when the IRS discovered that no taxes had been paid on the ill-got-ten gains, discovered in a safe-deposit box, the dealer committed suicide. *Served him right,* was the almost disinterested local verdict.

One night, after we had been visiting in town and getting groceries and meat from our locker in the locker plant, our Plymouth stalled on the Union Pacific railroad tracks.

We had waited for two trains to cross: there was quite a bit of fast activity on the rails then, during and just after the war years. The bells had stopped ringing at the crossing when we started to cross, but the car stalled; and almost immediately the bells began again and we looked up to see the terribly bright headlight of another train and heard the insistent screaming of its whistle. There were seven of us in the car: father, mother, two brothers, a sister, a new hired man, and I. Dad tried the starter once. It didn't work. I can still hear his *Get out!* The front passenger door generally stuck on the old Plymouth (there were no new cars during the war years), but it opened for my mother carrying little brother. I think my sister was in the front seat too. My other brother was sleeping in the back seat. He came running out as we started back to get him. He was small, and under other circumstances, seeing him charging full tilt though the open rear car door would have been funny, but on this occasion we were all just relieved that something woke him, perhaps the lack of warmth from being in a crowded back seat. We stood by the side of the track to watch our only means of transportation at that time, other than our tractors and grain truck, get dragged down the track and explode. The train managed to stop a half mile down the track. It had been doing seventy miles and hour. We had thirty seconds to get out after the bells rang. So far as the town was concerned, we were all dead, the evidence being the meat ground up and scattered along the tracks. Of course, the meat was the frozen meat we had picked up from the locker plant, which was the place where meat was kept before the home freezer appeared. My concern, the concern of a very young man, was for the bamboo fly rod for which I had just paid an atrocious (at that time) $25, and which was in the trunk of the car. The fly rod had come from the safe of a machinery dealer in town—not the dealer mentioned before—and I felt he had taken advantage of wartime scarcity. It was broken. A skinning knife my father had given me was in the glove compartment. It was intact. I have it still.

The war had barely ended then, and there were no new cars yet, and no new fly rods. To replace the Plymouth, we found a used Dodge, which took more money "under the table," while we waited for our name to come up on the list of those waiting for new cars. I was able to make a shortened fly rod from the parts that were left. This was important as we planned a trip to Yellowstone Park in

Wyoming for our first post-war vacation and some fly fishing. My father had tried fly fishing before the war on a trip to Colorado. We needed the trip, but for a very long time my family grew very silent at the sound of any train whistle. If it rained, or if we were between chores, or if we had no equipment that needed immediate repair, Dad took us fishing. Right after the war he bought one of the first boats in the area, as boats became feasible with the filling of the reservoirs behind the dams on the Plattes. The boat was with us many years, a fourteen foot, "strip boat" with a covered bow, a" Wolverine." The motor, a used Martin, a rather obscure brand, never ran properly, and we were finally able to replace it with a new Evinrude. Mother would fry chicken and make potato salad, and we would trailer the boat to Sutherland Reservoir or Lake McConaughy for fishing and a picnic. The trailer was a curious affair with belting and a winch. To retrieve it from the water you drove the boat close, put the belting under it, and cranked it up. It was the only boat my father ever had. He still had it when my sister, who is eight years younger than I, got married, and I can remember a family trip to Welfleet Lake which included her husband. Somehow I ended up with it. I used it for a couple of years, but eventually it needed repairs I didn't have time for, and I sold it and the trailer for fifty dollars.

In later years, when my brothers and I were gone, my father equipped the farm and cattle operation with machinery that allowed him, with occasional help from my mother, to handle the entire operation pretty much by himself. Limiting the operation to cattle and wheat allowed time for a couple of fly fishing days to Yellowstone Park every summer after the wheat harvest. He had time to be a co-op board member and visit with men in town. His black hair became salt and pepper and almost white; he gained some weight. When he died of complications from what should have been the most simple of surgeries, the heifers were in the pasture behind the house, and the granaries were full. He lived as he had wanted, never wanting to be or do anything else. You knew that, without his ever having said so.

Mother was a nineteen year old country school teacher when she married my father. Indeed, her school was District Number 23, the same school I walked to and from when the mallards were overhead. She was sixteen when she went to college, when just going to college for a girl from the country was something to be remarked. Her two sisters also went to college in their respective progression, which demonstrated the place of education in the minds and hearts of their German immigrant parents from Russia, who had to learn a new language and new way of life and quite possibly a new way of thinking when they chose to leave the orchards along the Volga for the valleys of the Plattes. Education had not the same priority in the my father's family, however, where only one or two of ten so much as finished high school.

Mother was born in Lincoln, the first of three sisters. Like my father she spoke German before she learned English. I know less of the circumstances of her family's moving to the north valley than I do of my father's. The farm her family lived on was across the road from the farm my father's family worked, but I have no idea how much communication occurred between the families before my mother and father married. An irony and perpetual source of amusement and trouble to me has been that my mother and father shared the same last name, and not a very common name then. The families could never establish a blood relationship, no matter how far back they went in recapitulating family history. But for me it always meant saying, Yes, *that is my mother's maiden name, the same as my father's name; and so far as I know, there's never been an idiot in the bunch.* Much later, when I met residents of Pennsylvania who carried the Reitz name and said they had been in the country before the revolution, I speculated that there must have been a smart branch and a dumb branch of the family. When they all left Bavaria, the smart branch came to America while the dumb branch went to Russia; and we were obviously members of the dumb branch. At least, when you call Pennsylvania, whomever you talk with can pronounce your name right.

So far as I can tell, my mother's family got to Paxton when she was about eight. She died at eighty-eight and always said she had been eighty years in the community. I know she graduated from Paxton High School when she was sixteen and started studies at the University of Nebraska at the same age. What I know of her college experience is limited to knowing she had a job, walked twenty blocks to the campus, and took German as her second language, which she said did require some study as there was a difference between the literary High German of the curriculum and the Low German dialect she knew. She stayed two years to complete what was called the "Normal Program" for teachers, and so far as I could tell, met, or at least began dating my father when she was teaching at School District 23. She said my father was a good dancer and a gentleman, and they went to dances in his Pontiac across country in the moonlight because there were no fences yet, and navigation was by memory and starlight rather than by road. He was twenty-four and she was nineteen when they were married in a German Lutheran church (maybe the same church I was baptized in; I do not know) in a big German celebration. Their wedding picture shows a very handsome couple, he with thick black hair, combed straight back with a part in the middle, she with a rather short wedding dress and bobbed blonde hairdo—all in the flapper style of the time.

My mother was a maker and keeper of journals: when she died I found thirty-one of various kinds, including one with a rather detailed description of the honeymoon trip, which took them from Paxton, Nebraska to Yosemite Park in California, an adventure over dirt roads much of the way, to the exhaustion of their monetary goods, down to a ten-dollar gold piece. There were relatives in California. A photograph of the couple in Yosemite shows them in breeches and high lace boots. The journals in aggregate are concerned mostly with the weather, the crops, the cattle, economic concerns, and events with relatives. There are few remarks of personal nature until she was older: then notations concerning her painful progress toward advanced osteoporosis occur. Many of the diaries are notations on small, desk-sized calendars, but a few are actually small notebooks. My mother was a prodigious writer of letters: my replies to correspondence just to me while I was in college filled a metal picnic basket. She kept in touch with most of the family, with letters, notes, and gifts on all the special occasions. She saved a large collection of old Valentines and Christmas cards. She was the person who kept family relationships and social connections alive; she was the glue that kept personal connections close and predictable, especially after my father died. I will probably, whether it is right or wrong to think so, always think of the maker of connections as a woman's special talent.

My mother was a reader as well as a writer, and our house was always supplied with magazines and books. *Colliers, The Saturday Evening Post, National Geographic,* and one I think was called *The American* or something like that were always regularly there. Language was important in our house, though only English was spoken, unless my parents wanted to discuss something in private. They made no attempt to teach us German, something I have regretted; but English was the language of America so far as they were concerned. They had, after all, been born in America, and German was an accident of childhood. We had many vocabulary discussions, which were always settled with Mother's college dictionary, which by the time of our growing up on the fourth farm was pretty well worn out.

Reading was considered an after-chore activity, however; and I can remember many times saying, *I'll get to it after I finish this chapter,* or *Just a minute 'till I finish this article.* Sometimes I actually got to finish the chapter or article.

How my parents found time for anything but work seems amazing to me now. They always had a large garden, and the garden always included a huge flower bed beside the strawberries, beans, peas, tomatoes, carrots, lettuce, and the few rows of sweet corn. My parents shared the gardening, and I wasn't left out either; but much of the work, especially in the gladiolas, snapdragons, zinnias, bachelor buttons, fell to Mother. My father loved roses (perhaps it had something to do with my mother's name), and always had rose bushes he took care of. Mother also kept the house and sun porch full of potted plants. When we "sold her out," as one of her neighbors put it, selling on site by auction everything in her house in town, a Christmas cactus that must have been fifty years old, at least, was part of the sale.

Our electricity in the first years on that farm was a fourteen volt system limited by the capacity of our three or four banks of wet-cell batteries and the generating power of our wind-charger, (Win-Charger it said on the tail fin). We could check on the power available by looking at the colored balls in the batteries. When completely charged we had a green ball up; a yellow ball meant we should hope for wind; a red ball meant the lights would be dim at best, and it was time to make certain the kerosene lamps or Coleman lanterns had fuel in them. When the wind didn't blow we used the kerosene lamps or a Coleman lantern and pumped water to the water tank with a gasoline powered "pump jack." The absence of regular electricity made Mother's work harder in many ways. Monday's were wash days. Wash days required filling the big, copper boiler with water and heating it on the stove in the washhouse. My father would fill the boiler, put it on the stove, and get the stove going with wood or corn cobs or coal to heat the water. The washing machine was powered by a small gasoline engine that was vented out of the side of the washhouse, and the put-put-put sound of wash days is still part of the memory. Mother made the soap too, a lye concoction that took advantage of products from the animals we killed and I don't know what else. The soap was soft and easy to carve, and one of the snowed-in activities when we were young was to carve the soap into animals or machinery. The carvings didn't waste any soap, as they became part of the clothes washing anyway. I don't know if the soap had anything to do with my discomfort whenever I put on clean underwear after the Saturday bath. My skin would crawl. The clothes all had to be hung on the clotheslines outdoors, which was fine and made them smell like sunshine, except in winter the clothes all froze, and we brought them in to the house like cordwood and had to dry them inside. We had an assortment of wooden racks for that. One of our winter jobs as youngsters was to bring in the clothes. Even frozen they smelled good.

Mother's clothes iron then ran on kerosene. You had to pump it up like the Coleman lantern. She also had flat irons she could heat on the stove, heavy, ugly things that in later times would make good door stops.

We eventually lost the limited electricity provided by the Win-Charger too. I was in the south field summer tilling on the Oliver crawler, which had a top speed of four and a half miles an hour, when I looked up to see a thunderstorm-created wall of dust hundreds of feet high coming rapidly from the west. I had never seen anything like it, and never again saw anything like it. It must have been what the dust bowl winds looked like. I knew I had to get to the house, as no one else was at home at the time, and besides I didn't know how dangerous it was to remain in the field. By the time I got to the house I had to put my bandana over my face to breathe. I was too late anyway. I would have turned the Win-Charger off, that is, pulled in the tail so that the propeller couldn't turn; but by the time I got there it had been torn off. We never repaired it, getting along without electricity until the REA came through.

My mother was a fine baker. Bread and pie smells frequently filled the house. I didn't know until I went to college that there was a better way than frying or roasting to prepare meat, however. Steaks and sausage, which my father made by the tubful after butchering, were fried—completely, thoroughly. Pork chops especially were given the complete treatment. Fowl experienced better treatment: our turkeys were all well-roasted and the many fryers we raised, always young and tender when prepared were something special; but I could never get my mother to go easy on the wild duck, though she would fill the duck's cavity with apples to retain some moisture. But they too were always very, very well done. Although we had the very best steak, "baby beef" from animals raised with our 4-H beef projects, I didn't know about rare steak until I left home.

It would be a mistake, though, to think of beef or duck handling as typical of Mother's culinary ability. She made wonderful breads and pastries. She entertained thirty friends and relatives at a time on special days: on Thanksgiving there might be favors that looked like little turkeys made of several sizes of gumdrops and cut-outs to complete the illusion; there would be appetizers of fruit cocktail, and desert might include baked Alaska. No meal was complete without dessert, pies from fruit to chiffon, cakes from angel food to upside down. She made marvelous German or Russian dishes—some dishes we always thought German were probably Russian. A favorite for breakfast was "blina," a large crepe-thin pancake we covered with butter and syrup and rolled up. You ate it by cutting perpendicularly across the roll. Kuchen or kucha, as it was usually called was a staple: the topping could be anything from the frequent buttery crumbles to cherries or "yagada." "Yagada" was a small, black, berry that had to be planted once only. From then on it grew in gardens voluntarily. I have no idea where it came from or what it really is or if I spelled it correctly. It has a special sweet-tart flavor and was a favorite not only on the kuchen, but also in the "gilfilten," also called "runza" in our family, a wonderful filled concoction that could be everything from cheese to potatoes to cherries to "yagada." A dough surrounded these fillings, was usually formed in triangles, deep fried, and covered with a buttery glaze. There was "grebble," an elongated raised donut kind of bread always rolled in sugar. We had "kartoffel and glace," and butter balls in noodles soup (I never heard any German for that). Liver and cream was a favorite, meaning the liver was poached in the cream. Bread then soaked up the cream. My mother made "kraut brot," a cabbage filled bread thing, and we bought what were called "krautburgers" whenever we were in Scottsbluff. My father made not only German sausage but liver sausage also. He made it by the wash tub full. We had a large cast iron press for filling the casing with sausage. We blew up the salty casings by mouth before stripping them on the press. My mother would fry the circles of sausage for breakfast. We had "sweet breads," and liver, and heart—no kidneys though; they were never part of the larder. Bacon was usually in large slabs on the skin, the thick kind, for when we had swine we had them butchered and cured to our specifications. Mother made two kinds of cheese when we had our own milk. Sour kraut came from the Grandpa Fred farm in the early days. Grandpa Fred had a wooden trough with a blade in it to slide the cabbage across and cut it into ribbons and large crocks to keep everything in. They also made pickles and pickled watermelon. Easter at home was always commemorated with dozens of colored eggs, and Easter morning was always celebrated by the break-the-end-of-the-egg contest during which sharp ends were tested against sharp ends and blunt were tested against blunt. A good, strong egg would last several rounds. Food was important, and meals became the stuff of reminiscence.

Easter also meant that everyone went to church in new clothes, Mother in a new hat and dress, the rest of us in new outfits, or at least new shoes. New, bright clothes were as much a spring ritual as new leaves on the trees or newborn claves or red-winged blackbirds making their musical squeaking-door rasping noises from old cattails.

Shortly before D-Day my little brother was born, thirteen years after my own arrival elsewhere, which meant the household in the fourth farm came to six. One could almost define my mother by the prodigious labors of a farm woman—family, house, yard, sometimes, in the later years, when we were all gone, the corral too, where she would help move the livestock, or during the winter feeding she would drive the pickup while my father cut open and scattered the bales of hay for the cattle. In my family, however, women were rarely asked to help in the field or corral. They never milked cows or drove tractors or handled horses.

But house work and farm chores would hardly define my mother. She still sang around the house. She sang with the church choir, taught Sunday School, belonged to the local garden club, managed all of our many social affairs—and figured the hay tonnage for her in-laws, as the one with the education to do such things. She sometimes remarked that her ability to figure the hay was her main redeeming virtue so far as her father-in-law was concerned. She found time to read, play the piano and the violin. Her reading was not confined to the magazines and the materials she used to get ready for church or teach Sunday School. I can remember with some amusement her inveighing against *Lady Chatterley's Lover,* but she read it all. She was outspoken enough to cause occasional resentments and certainly too smart for some parts of the family, so her feelings were hurt on more than one occasion. I have always regretted being the cause of some of those hurt feelings as I grew older and insisted upon my own independence, usually in religious matters. It takes some experience not to be needlessly assertive. But mother would control things if she could, as do many strong mothers; and at some point sons will assert their independence.

Mother was in charge of dressing the dozens of fryers we raised every year in the earlier years, some for our own use, some for sale in town. She would decide when and how many, and it was often my job to catch and kill them, sometimes as many as forty at a time. I would decapitate them with a beet knife with the pick broken off, a relic of the earlier beet farming years. There would be chickens jumping all over the lawn near the wash house: jumping "like chickens with their heads cut off" was an expression that never had to be explained to us. The chickens were then dipped in boiling water to loosen the feathers and plucked. The smell of wet feathers is a pungent, and not pleasant, memory. Fried chicken is a pleasant summertime memory, however: we always dressed them young, around a tender two and a half pounds, so that even the "scratchers" (feet) were tender.

During the first years on the fourth farm we had enough eggs to sell them by the crate and sufficient milk to sell cream by the "cream-can" full, hauling them to the railroad station to be shipped. That meant using the separator in the basement twice a day, first by hand cranking it and finally with a fourteen volt electric motor. The electric motor did not have enough power to start the separator; you had to do that by hand, and then the motor would take over. The evening separator operation was always after dark. We churned our own butter, and mother would make bricks of it with a wooden form.

We sold some of that in town, along with thick, "whipping" cream that didn't go into the cans to be shipped. We cultured, "made clabbered" milk for ourselves and for the hogs. Farm days began at first light, or even before, and ended after dark usually. We didn't count the hours. Eventually, as we became more specialized with crops and cattle, we got rid of the milk cows and hogs and kept only enough chickens for our own use. By the time my brothers and sister and I left home, the chores had been pared and the machinery modernized so that my mother and father could manage the operation by themselves most of the time. My father no longer combined at wheat harvest, for example; he hired traveling crews to do it. Instead of driving the cattle north to pasture in spring he had them trucked, and trucked home in fall too.

The Lutheran Church was a major part of my mother's life; indeed it was the focus of many of our activities, and the activities of the "hometown." Paxton had not only a very active Lutheran congregation at that time, but also a large Catholic contingent and a fair number of Methodists. The Lutherans seemed to inhabit the north, the Catholics the south, and the Methodists the town. We had a large Mennonite community to our west. They had their own church, out in the country. They spoke a different German dialect, when they spoke German; but mainly they were as reluctant to use the old language as were our own parents, at least around us. I don't know what language they used in their church, but they were prosperous farmers, raising mostly corn and wheat, went to the same schools we did, and were completely indistinguishable from anyone else in our community. We traded labor and machinery with them sometimes.

Before the REA (Rural Electrification Administration) came through we heated water in the kitchen with a tank connected to our "woodstove." (Mainly we burned cobs or coal.) We had a propane gas refrigerator by then, and on that farm we had installed a toilet and bathtub inside. We had water pressure from the windmill's elevated storage tank, which made indoor plumbing possible. We drove the pipes underground with a lever-type device that saved us from having to make ditches everywhere. We dug and installed the septic system. We did have to dig the trench for the drain field, which was actually the wheat field south of the house. The house had no central heat: we installed a propane fired furnace in the dining room and heater in the bathroom. After the propane furnace came a propane fired kitchen range too, heat from the old, iron woodstove being no longer necessary. Years later, with the coming of REA, home freezers replaced the locker in town, and a washer and dryer reduced the washhouse to storage. We always improved the places we rented, inside and out. Sometimes the landlord shared in the expense, sometimes not. We had a large extension to the house built. It became the living room. We had the house insulated and added windows to the porch to make the sun porch. My parents lived in that house on that farm for more than thirty years and that "place," as any farm was called then, was the "homeplace" to all of us for a long time. My father, especially, was always amused by city folk, who called a house the ranch rather than the ranchhouse, or confused a farmhouse for a farm: the ranch was the land itself as was the farm. Land around the house was the farm yard, which also might include the garage and some granaries and places to park the cars and trucks and other machinery. After the REA came in we had a yard light, which at night lighted most of the area all night long, for convenience and security. Corrals and pens were not part of the "yard" though often immediately adjacent, and included the barns and other buildings, like hog houses. There were feed bunks and stock tanks and wooden windbreaks on the north and the west. In winter we put a propane heater in the main stock tank. We planted a long line of Chinese elms and some cedars on the north side of the garden near the house all the way down past the wooden windbreaks of the corrals. We had to carry water to them to get them started, but over the years they provided important shelter for us and the animals in the pens and corrals, and places for the pheasants to roost and a secure route to water at the stock tank when the lagoons were dry and in winter.

I participated in the usual church functions, catechism at fourteen, the choir, an occasional solo even; but church mainly gave me a headache. I liked the music well enough and the socializing and even the ethical concernment, but the doom and gloom and piety assumed an arrogance, even then, that were both amusing and irritating to my sense of things. It didn't help that home room in high school was in the library, and one day I noticed I was sitting beside a collection of the works of Charles Darwin, a man who's name had been taken in vain several times by our Lutheran minister. So I read the books, straight through: *Origin of Species, Descent of Man,* and a treatise on the earth worm, that I understand is still considered authoritative. I discovered that the minister had apparently never read Darwin, who was at least as "Godly" as the minister himself. Besides, I had already read through the set of Earnest Thomson Seton that was also near my home room desk and was well aware of a world of curiosity and intellectual discipline far removed (it seemed to me) from narrow Protestant gloom. Reading Darwin was epiphany of a different sort for me, and I never again accepted the kind of

Aristotelian logic (as I learned to think of it later) dear to official piety. My increasing skepticism caused my mother some concern, even though I continued a church association in college, doing a little solo work and enjoying the collegiate Luther Club (I think it was called). The mountain "retreats" were pleasant, especially when one's girl friend was part of the group.

It's a bit surprising to me now that the school library in our small town had such books as Darwin's and Seton's, given the rather narrow range of speculation outside the conventions of Lutheran, Methodist, and Catholic—weather, crops, cattle, and horses. High school sports were a big deal (before we used the term), and I understand they played poker in Ole's back room, as did some of my high school buddies on road trips for sports or music or academic contests. There were the public dances and ice skating parties. The boys drove around on Saturday nights. I found the public dances, with their drunken, overt sexuality, stifling and crude, though I did enjoy watching the band's pianist; and riding around on Saturday nights with high school boys was a bore, though I liked the skating and high school dances. Obviously, prodigious events happened in my town that I, who lived mainly in the country anyway, never knew anything about. No doubt, I was as guilty of teenage arrogance as the next person and lived in as narrow a world. But as long as my parents were there I kept in touch, coming back for holidays, weddings, funerals, and occasional bird hunts with my father and brothers. For a few years, immediately after the military service time, I lived with my own family in nearby Ogallala. This time allowed my wife and daughters to become acquainted with in-laws, grandparents, and farm and ranch life. It has had a permanent effect on all of us.

It was on this place my parents lived after we were all long gone. It was from here my father went to the hospital to die, with the heifers of the year in the pasture behind the house, the granaries full, and the main herd still in the sandhills. I was leaning on my bedroom window sill, looking out of that upstairs window of my Wyoming home at four in the morning—I do not know why—on the August night when the call came. Dad had died in the hospital of pneumonia. He had gone home after a hernia repair and never felt well. He had waited too long to go back to the hospital. I was not ready for him to die; but one learns at such times that even one's parents die on their own terms.

After the funeral I drove my daughters around the north valley and pointed out the places of memory, the first little house I remembered, where the first farm was and just down the road the house where brother Mike was born and Grandpa Mike died; the farm across the road that was farmed by my Grandpa Fred and Grandma Katherine and by their Grandpa Chris in those first years; the sandpit where we ice skated and later fly fished for bass and bluegills with "poppers"; the road north to the sandhill pasture; the Lute farm my uncles John and Fred worked; and all the farms on the way back to town, which I could name by their owners or inhabitants. *Gosh, Dad,* one of my daughters said, *You have roots.*

It was there on the fourth farm that the inevitable farm sale took place, and my mother moved to town, to a house where she could see the Lutheran church to the west, a church that had in large part been built by the congregation—I can remember spending most of a day helping to nail down the sub-floor. The Catholic church was across and down the street, and the between-the-rivers sandhills were just one house to the north. First, she toured Europe with her sister and husband, my Aunt Esther and Uncle Roger, and then settled in to complain for years about the emptiness of a life without my father and the unfairness of his missing the last few months before their fiftieth anniversary. She planted flowers and tended them even when stooping caused excruciating pain from the ever worsening degeneration of her spine. She kept up her large correspondence and church involvement and continued to cheer for the Nebraska Cornhuskers. She had great scrabble sessions with a special friend, one of the few of her acquaintance with whom she could share conjecture and ideas outside the universal topics of weather, crops, cattle, and grandchildren. She was visited frequently by friends and relatives, and the Paxton house became the gathering place for the immediate family of sons, daughters-in-law, daughter and son-in-law, and grandchildren during Christmases, Memorial Days, Fourth of July's and fishing and hunting seasons. There were plenty of beds and couches for sleeping, and Mother always had a long list of "chores" around the house that she needed help with. Neighbors and relatives looked after her and brought her the mail when she could no longer walk to the mailbox.

She was there seventeen years and no longer able to drive her Chevy to get to the beauty shop for her weekly hairdo before she resentfully moved to a care facility in North Platte. "Nursing home" was not a happy destination for any of her generation, even if it was called "Retirement Village." She always resented being there; but her children were all elsewhere or in transition, and there was no way any of us could have taken care of someone who could no longer get up or down stairs or even bathe herself, who was now suffering not only from advanced osteoporosis but a congestive heart condition. I'm sure we were all roundly despised, at least for a time, for not somehow taking care of her "as they did in the old days." I had already retired, and my wife and I had come down for our annual fall visit on our way south for the winter when we found her in the terrible pain. A trip to the emergency room in North Platte confirmed four broken verte-brae. Our three day visit became three weeks as we sold the house and after that its contents at auction on the site—"sold her out" in the words of the neighbor.

After the sale I went alone to the south side farm and drove though that part with the two tracks and the original prairie grass. A cousin farms the place now, and a hired man lives in our old house. I flushed a sharptail grouse there in the old grass, a bird that we had before seen on the south side only in winter, when the sharptails and prairie chickens migrated from the sandhills. In times past this had been their regular habitat also. It was as if time and life had come full circle.

Mother's keen intelligence never failed: she read, crocheted, worked her daily crossword puzzles, enjoyed her favorite television program, "Jeopardy," without fail—indeed, even before the wheelchair became too much, she had her evening meal brought in rather than miss the program. We kept in touch, she by letter, I by phone every week. We visited every spring and fall. One February evening she called to say she was tired and she loved me. The next morning my "little" brother, who was now a veterinary and decorated Viet Nam veteran helicopter pilot, called to say, *Mom's gone, in her sleep.* She had been there almost three years. The director said, *We miss Rosa; she has been mentor to us all.* I miss keenly her letters and our weekly phone conversations. I suppose that everyone must learn for oneself that the loss of parents forever diminishes life, that the regret of aging is communal as well as personal; and that there is no help for it. Chris and Rosa, father and mother, ever synonymous with *home*—

I suppose my years growing up on the fourth farm would be called the forma-tive years, as it is after those years that I left, and it was during those years I ended the one-room-school-house experience and went to school in town; and then to college and other things, but my feeling for what I call home is not so simple. For example, I had been to two schools in town, Paxton and Sutherland, before the country school experience. Nearly everything I can remember seems to have some relationship to what I became, and I seem to be able to remember a lot, though not nearly as much as I would like. What I became is important mainly as the only means I have to preserve what I want remembered and celebrated—the time and place and persons and good fortune in having a place that defines home. And the place covers the entire area, not just the fourth farm but the first farms too; and the persons include the extended family as well as the immediate. Though we lived eight and a half miles from town it would be a mistake to think of our lives in any way isolated. We were in constant, if not daily, association with relatives, neighbors, friends, hired men, hired girls, the congregation at church, members of 4-H, local and not-so-local merchants and business men and women, doctors, dentists, the veterinary who had to make occasional trips when something came up we couldn't handle ourselves.

The time, of course, is finite, like everything else. Only the place lives on, though not as it was. The country then was composed of smaller farms and ranches and smaller towns, some of them today smaller still. Few roads were paved. The railroad was more important for hauling persons and cattle than hauling coal, and the engines were coal fired though diesel-electric was beginning to replace them. No jetliners painted the sky. Towns had noon sirens, and though we lived eight and a half miles from town by road, we could hear the noon siren from Paxton when conditions were just right; but most folks who lived in the country knew noon by the sun's position, or rather, by the shadows cast by the fence posts. In any event, "home" centers on the fourth farm and, and though it was the last place in sequence, it owns the center in memory and in the physical and intellectual universe that someone else has called "song of myself."

Living three or four miles almost due east of our place were Uncle Ray and Aunt Anna, Anna being one of my father's sisters. It always seemed to me that our relationship was more taken for granted than close, although it was obvious that I was not nor would have been privy to all of the adult commerce that had to have taken place over the years. I considered uncle Ray to be brusque, if not aloof, not given to much concern for anything except wheat, corn, and hay for the cows in that mixed rich soil, sandy soil, grassy hills country of western Nebraska that we all called home—and an occasional new Chevrolet when they were again manufactured. He and Aunt Anna owned their farm, and I remember an occasional remark about it when the yearly rent came due, ours going to the banker, what would have been his going for payments on his land or another new Chevy. In time Uncle Ray became a County Commissioner—this after I was gone—and the sandy, sometimes muddy road that came near our places was paved. Uncle Ray had a flat, matter-of-fact way of speaking, when he spoke, and his laugh was ironic.

One day while I was walking the regular, rather than my usual, cross-country route home from District 23, Uncle Ray was waiting for me at the end of his lane. *Here*, he said. He handed me a box of .410-short shotgun shells, especially hard to find in those times. Completely surprised, but having grown up in the company of men, working with men and doing a "man's work" from the age of seven, although I was probably around twelve at that point, I responded as I had heard men respond when surprised by any kindness. *How am I supposed to take this?* I said.

Take it anyway you want, he said. I managed a thanks anyway, but I recognized a part of my uncle I had not expected along with the part that seemed entirely in character. That there was communication between my father and uncle of which I was totally unaware was also obvious. Though I can name my cousins by Uncle Ray and Aunt Anna, I never associated with them. The cousins we were close to were all on my mother's side, no doubt because we spent more time with her two sisters' families.

The District 23 schoolhouse, the proverbial one-room schoolhouse in the country, was actually two rooms; the building was white, not the color of poetry. You entered the little room, which was little more than an entry, except it held the water crock, which had to be filled every day. We hung our coats and took off our overshoes there. That room was unheated, but the water didn't quite freeze as there was enough heat from the big room, the classroom itself, with its black and white pictures of Washington and Lincoln. The toilet was a wooden stand-alone privy behind the schoolhouse. Sometimes as many as eight students, who could represent grades one through eight, attended. Sometimes there was only my brother Mike. When things were lively, the students included Sam, and sisters Ronda and Judy. Ronda was blonde, fair, and the elder; Judy was an attractive brunette, with smooth, olive skin, and fine hairs on her upper lip. When I remember her most she was already dating a truck driver in town, and one memorable recess, when we were outside between the privy and the schoolhouse she showed me a gift from her truck driver—a little rubber man in a barrel who when pushed through the barrel displayed a huge penis. I don't remember if I was impressed more by the size of the penis or with Judy herself, to whom, obviously, I should have paid more attention.

Our teachers, none of whose names I remember, were all "normal school" graduates, that is to say, they had two years of college in a college of education like Kearney College. I remember only a couple of incidents with them, one a cute young "schoolmarm" whose boyfriend picked her up on Friday afternoons. Actually, what I remember is how close shaven he was and how friendly she was too him. The other teacher I remember was homely and a bit sour. My most memorable encounter with her was during our hygiene class, which was really quite good, with a pretty thorough study of human anatomy and a good textbook. She insisted the pupil of the human eye was an aperture, or something like that, even when I showed her in the encyclopedia that that was not so. As a Catholic, she also insisted that fish was not meat, a pretty stupid distinction to a Lutheran farm-ranch kid. But they didn't hurt us any: we had good texts and the advantage of hearing every class of every grade, so we were always moving in two directions at once, no matter what grade we were in—reviewing and learning new things at the same time.

In springtime the large lagoon across the road filled, and the shorebirds came, some with a plaintive *Killdeer, Killdeer*, and the distinctive smell of wet pasture mingled with the smell of eraser dust and wet coats. It was springtime when Judy showed me the rubber man in the barrel and Sam disappeared frequently, probably to help with the spring field work. Sam went to high school in a Model A that I once got to drive—very loose steering, wandered all over the road. He got cozy with Jane, who told me my first dirty joke—though these days it would hardly qualify—about berry picking and a glove compartment, this on a basketball bus trip. Last time I saw Sam, at one of the high school reunions held every fifth year, he was as friendly as ever, and drunk.

If I walked or biked the main road home I passed an old country church I was to learn might have been the German-Lutheran church in which I was baptized. The church had been unused for years, but not a window had been broken, and although the door had never been locked the foot-pumped church organ was still there, and still worked. I know because I tried it. At some point the church disappeared, as did the District 23 schoolhouse, and after I graduated from high school with my class of twelve, the high school building was torn down, and although I looked for it's location once while visiting my mother, I could not be sure I ever found it, though I had attended school there from kindergarten though most of the third grade and again through high school. It had been my mother's high school too, and eventually she became its oldest, or one of its oldest, alumna. I used to remark that all the institutions of my growing up had disappeared, including the brick house in North Platte that served as the hospital I was born in, and that it was a good thing I went to college or I would have left no institutions standing.

The land changed too. Most of the "black root" prairie was plowed and turned from pasture into farmland for dry land farming. Then wells were drilled and hundreds of "pivots," irrigation systems that watered a quarter section with a circular motion from a central well, were installed. For a time the crops that pivots produced were government subsidized and many pivots were placed where they did not belong, lowering the water table, even in the sandhills where we ran the cattle, country in which every previous farming venture had ended in disaster. The sandhills were full of "blow outs," plots where farming had been tried and given up for lack of moisture; and with no ground cover the sand blew when the wind blew, contributing to the great dust bowl of history. Left alone the blowouts took forty years to recover the grasses that held them in the first place. They were a good source of arrowheads, and my father walked those on our pastures regularly, both to check the recovery and look for the flint signs of the past.

Judging from the numbers of missile points and the huge area over which they were found, humans had been there before, if not in vast numbers. for vast periods of time.

Definitive as it was to my growing up and as important as it was to the sense of myself and of everything that was or became important to me, I do not forget that the fourth farm itself was a place of hard work, uncertainty, and occasional disappointment. A semi-desert, which is what the shortgrass prairie is, defines itself by the extremes of a continental climate as well as the extremes of a relatively high semi-desert: the wind is so constant that calm or merely breezy days are remarked, as are really nice days. Most of the time it is too cold or too hot. Crops get hailed to the ground some years, and the hail destroys the gardens with their vegetable and flowers too. My family was made of the kind of stuff that gathered the hailstones for the ice cream freezer—*Might as well make the best of it.* In the books I read then were trees and water. Any trees we had we had to plant, and our surface water was, until the reservoirs came, limited to our seasonal lagoons and the two Plattes, some miles distant. Roads were either wash-boarded rough and dusty or smooth and muddy. As a teenager I swore I would leave the place and never come back.

Sibling relationships were not always ideal either. A vacation trip to the Black Hills to see Mount Rushmore and the other South Dakota sights is as memorable for sibling squabbling as much as for pretty mountains, lakes, and stone faces. I can remember how awful it was and my surprise that my parents paid no attention. What I would call "little brother logic" is perfectly illustrated by an event I can recall after more that sixty years. I had gone through the gate in the fence that surrounded the house, with its lawn and gardens. We had to have a fence to keep our free-roaming chickens out. I turned around to discover I was being followed by small first brother, who hadn't bothered to close the gate. *Why didn't you close the gate?* I remember saying.

The reply: *I didn't open it.*

There was the time I went to my taxidermy supplies, which I kept in an old desk in the basement, to find the wires I used, which were normally straight as they needed to be to perform their proper function, bent and twisted. Brother had got even for something—I have not idea what, and don't think I knew then.

He got into parent trouble for that one though. In later years I learned that being used by parents as an example does not endear one to one's brothers either, but I suppose that is just another part of being first son.

The reservoirs did make our semi-desert life more interesting and more tolerable to a young man whose reading was usually full of water and trees. Zane Grey's *Ken Ward in the Jungle,* for instance, had been an early favorite of mine—I must have read it four times. It was a book he had written for boys about a young man hunting the Mexican jungle, lots of water, lots of trees, lots of exotic animals—very different from our semi-desert. (When I mentioned Zane Grey to the new high school English teacher I was informed that he had no "literary" rank—my first run-in with the kind of snobbery common to what would become one of my own fields of interest.)

Anyway, with the filling of the reservoirs, we were able to boat and fish, when the wind did not blow too hard, anyway. Wind could ruin things: I remember distinctly a weekend morning I had looked forward to all week. I put the top down on the Chevy convertible that I used to get to school, and drove alone to fish the big lake. By the time I got there the wind was blowing so hard I could fish the lee of a side dam only. I did manage to catch a crappie on a little red and white Dardevil, but the morning sticks in my mind still as a perfect example of perverse prairie weather, especially the wind, which I grew to hate. Wind meant that the dust from the machinery strangled you on the tractor, either all the time or while you were going in one direction, unless you were lucky enough to be summer-tilling a field with equipment that allowed you to choose your direction. You could do that with rod-weeder or a disk; you could not do that with a "one way," as we called the side disk or one-way plow. I came very near "dust pneumonia," as the doctor called it, coughing through most of my junior and senior years.

I had to quit football altogether as we played football on a dirt field, and had to leave the basketball floor for coughing spells. I did not stop coughing until I got to college. I should hate the memory of the place; but I don't. As the poet said, *we love the things we love for what they are*—I should add, when we have become mature enough to know what they are, and how they have affected what *we* are. Then too, sometimes we know in spite of ourselves because of wings and starry skies. (Of course the final irony is that I eventually moved to Wyoming.)

Usually, of course, the wind was a good thing. It pumped our water. For some years it made our electricity. It made the wheat especially beautiful when the wheat was green and tall and it rippled with a stiff breeze that moved it in undulating waves, rustling waves, as the stiff wheat beards scraped together. A breeze was especially welcome on a stifling summer day when tractor work included dust and flies and sweat bees from the pink, flowering growth in the now empty lagoons. It could feel good when one was lying in the shade under the grain truck waiting for the next load of wheat during harvest. One summer, home from college, I read Plato that way. By then, of course, I was as glad to get back to college as I was to get home. Where I went to college the wind didn't blow as much, except once a year, when it blew trees over and roofs off. In those years it was good both coming and going.

During all the years on the fourth farm I was old enough to spend long days on the tractors. Except in the earliest days we always had several tractors to choose from, depending upon the work to be done. One was a an Oliver crawler (like a Caterpillar) which could do heavy work but created the most dust, even after we fabricated and welded fenders for it. It was probably the main cause of my respiratory problem. Another Oliver made so much transmission noise I stuffed my ears with cotton. You couldn't just climb on a tractor and take off for the field. Gas or diesel were required; air cleaners had to be serviced; oil had to be checked and frequently changed. When you got to the machinery zirks had to be greased. We were not in the habit of carrying water, so were somewhat dehydrated by noon and even more so at suppertime. I would come in at suppertime coated with dust and stick my head under the hydrant outside near the kitchen door to get rid of the dust and cool off. Cold water on the wrists helped especially. But, dehydrated, I could not get enough to drink, even of the cold, green coolade my mother always had ready. Eventually, though, we caught on and began carrying canvass bags or burlap wrapped jugs that were self-cooling through evaporation, as we did at harvest time. We installed "Bumbershoots" (big umbrellas) on the tractors and made a special shade, which was more or less successful—we had to keep re-welding it because of the vibration created by the crawler. But many days were enjoyable, if not delightful: you were your own boss, controlled what went on, had the freedom of space and time to dream or think through. There were birds and animals to notice, along with their proclivities and peculiarities. You told time by shadows for dinner at noon and went in for supper before dark.

Before combines took over there was threshing time and corn shelling time, when the neighbors got together. Bundles of wheat or oats or barley had to be loaded into hayracks by hand. The hayracks (wagons) could be pulled by team or tractor as the transition from animal to machine continued, but the hand loading by pitchfork was still required—and then the off-loading into the threshing machine (separator to some). The bundles could weigh forty pounds or more and had to be lifted over the sides of the hayracks and thrown on top of the bundles already there. Sometimes a neighbor like myself was my off-loading companion, and we would see if we could pitch bundles into the machine fast enough to plug it up. *Ah, boys,* the separator operator would say.

At corn shelling time the shelling machine was moved next to the corn cribs and the neighbors gathered with their cob forks to feed the machine. It was backbreaking work and lasted until the cribs were empty. *Does a man's work,* was genuine praise for a fourteen-year old. Corn shelling left huge cob piles. Cobs made good fuel for the earlier stoves. Before I left home combines harvested all the grain; there was no more corn for us to shell; soon, where there was corn it was combined, and our stove used propane.

Once, after the big blizzard, the same neighborhood crew that shelled the corn brought their number ten or twelve scoops, the same tools they used for wheat, to clear a mile of road. We made the snow fly and cleared the road. Our work lasted only a day, as the wind came and blew it full again—worse, because it filled in the trench we made. That was before the eighth Army moved in an plowed us free, incidentally plowing down fences and chicken coops too. The Army was a mixed blessing. In some places, though, they dropped hay to the cattle from airplanes. I was a senior in high school that year and missed two months of school, one to drill the wheat, the other because of the blizzard.

Then there was that new English teacher when I finally got to school. We had an immediate misunderstanding when after one of her "lectures" she asked me why I didn't take notes. She was not amused when I repeated, word-for-word, what she had said. I learned later that a "friend" in town who had been "taking her out," had set me up. He was already in college, and soon we would be making the trip together. Why he thought it amusing to "warn her about Reitz," I never found out. Maybe it had something to do with his dating her—or maybe it was the math teacher—*Breasts like puppy dog ears*, he said.

My relationship to high school was important, as I have already said. I did a lot of growing up and learning there, or at least during those years, sang in music contests, debated, went to academic contests, played football and basketball, enjoyed the dances and many school events. It was a means to become familiar with other parts of the state as I traveled with the teams or through other high school activities. My first date was a school sponsored hayride outing with a girl who had worked as one of our hired girls and who got to high school a year before I did.

But school was never my whole life. I was engaged in a more important family endeavor, with "real work" to do too. And I knew from the beginning that high school was not the end for me but merely another phase in my going elsewhere. College was as much an assumption as was moving from one grade to another. That was not true for half the class, successful as it was, for whom high school was final. They stayed in the community to marry and work, or lived nearby. The community remained home to them in the literal sense.

Why that, rather extensive, part of the shortgrass prairie should be home to me in any sense might be something of a mystery if all I had to relate to was the fourth farm and the March mallards: after all, I was there only about seven years and an extra four summers, the college summers, and the last summer before going into the service for a couple of years. I was only seventeen when I left for college. My idea of home has to be related to an accumulated experience that led up to the March mallards. Surely the experience of the first three farms was essential, for those places too were a vital part of growing up in the semi-desert we called home. In a very real way the first years represent an age of innocence not only for me, but for my country as well.

The Sutherland Place

The third farm was sugar beets, potatoes, small grain, a small truck garden, lots of hay—and endless irrigation. It extended from the Union Pacific railroad tracks (so close to the house that the house shook with every train) to the South Platte River. Located at the very eastern edge of Sutherland, the farm extended east, the fields bordered by the railroad right-of-way on the north and a pasture and extensive hay fields on the south, the hay field extending to the river. A dirt road bordered the west side of the land, all the way to the river. Sutherland is not very far from the strip of sandhills between the north and south rivers, but the valley gets wider as you go east until the two Plattes converge just east of North Platte to form the main river.

If you were to follow the Platte River, when it becomes a single river, east to the ninety-eighth meridian, you would find you had entered a different Nebraska, for at the ninety-eighth meridian precipitation increases as if the line held some magic—actually the magic is that you would have finally passed the long rain shadow of the Rocky Mountains. If you looked at a map of railroads or roads in general, you would see a sudden increase in tracks and highways; and if you looked at a map of populations you would suddenly find bigger towns and Nebraska's only cities. Sutherland is in the Mountain Time Zone; North Platte, twenty miles east, is in the Central Time Zone. East of the ninety-eighth meridian are most of Nebraska's ninety-three counties, much smaller counties than those in the west. Western Nebraskans have on occasion threatened to join Wyoming, claiming they have been forgotten and slighted by the political power of the east, where the state capital is. Sutherland residents often go by North Platte time rather than having to calculate the hour's difference when they go to North Platte to see the doctor or dentist. My family simply got used to calculating the difference, for no matter where we lived in the area, Paxton or Sutherland, we had to be aware of the hour, as if we were always residents of one country doing major business in another.

The water for irrigation on the Sutherland place was supplied by an electric pump that provided a thousand gallons of ground water every hour. It was unbelievably cold. On some hot summer days I jumped into one of main ditches that

52

irrigated the lawn at the house but always jumped right back out as the water couldn't be tolerated for more than a few seconds. The pump was in a little building we called the "pump house" which had large window-like panels that opened upward to supply air to cool the electric motor, which ran constantly during irrigation periods. Sometimes my job was to stay at the pump house and monitor the motor. To make a really boring job more palatable I was paid to swat the big blue flies that hung around the pump house at a penny a piece. This was not just to give me something to do: for some reason my family really couldn't stand flies. Any that were unlucky enough to get into the house were pursued relentlessly. Grandma Molly could catch them by hand and smashed them with such serious vigor you thought of St. George and the dragon.

Because sugar beets were a major crop, we had a Mexican family working for us. They lived in the "beet house" south of the main house during the beet campaign, as it was called, and then returned to Texas. Taking care of sugar beets meant thinning, weeding, irrigating, and at harvest time, after the beets were pulled by machine, piling and loading them on trucks for their journey to the big pile from which trains would take them to the refinery. It was hard, hot, summer work until harvest time, and there were Mexican families all over the South Platte valley doing the work. We had a very nice family, and my father not only paid them for the beet work, but for irrigating and tilling also, which he taught them to do. I played cowboys and Indians with the boys during some evenings when the work was done, and they taught me how accurate sling shots could be—we all carried sling shots in our back pockets. When we played cowboys and Indians and they ambushed me or my brother, they never made their toy pistols say *Kkuuu, Kkuuu,* loudly, as was our way of firing; they said *Pow, Pow,* so softly that you almost weren't aware that you had just been shot. I never understood that. The only Spanish word they ever taught us was "andalay," which was a word we heard their parents use in the fields and meant "hurry up," we were told. I have since tried to find the word several times in my Spanish dictionary, but the closest I can come up with is "andar," which can mean "to run," but the conjugations I found don't include anything like "andalay." Recently I have learned the word is slang or idiom.

Potatoes were one of our important crops. My first experience with machinery was in cultivating potatoes. We still used horses in those times too; tractors had not yet taken over all the work. Potatoes required preparing the seed, which was a portion of the potato itself. You did that by slicing potatoes in sections, each section having at least one "eye." This was an early spring activity when it was still pretty cool, even cold. We did it inside one of the boxcar granaries. You could sit down doing this job, affixing a sharp beet knife between a slit in a board and pushing the potatoes against the blade. It was pleasant, social work, though messy. Potatoes had to be planted, cultivated, watched for "potato bugs," dug, sacked, loaded on trucks, and hauled to market. Market meant stores or potato chip factories, where you hoped to get two or three dollars for a hundred pounds but in bad times were lucky to settle for fifty cents. When the "spuds" weren't worth hauling to market we cooked them in a big iron pot and fed them to the hogs.

We raised lots of hogs on the Sutherland place, until they all got erysipelis and died. I don't remember how many pigs we lost—it may have been seventeen or it may have been seventy—but I do remember it as a major economic blow. This all happened about the time somebody named Wallace was causing a lot of angry talk around our place as he was drowning hogs to get rid of a surplus when some folks didn't have enough to eat. My family was always against any kind of government intervention in the farm business.

From the Sutherland Place we trailed our cattle herd thirty-five miles north to sandhill pasture in the spring, always driving them from horseback. I don't think we had family pasture then; I think we leased it. These were my first cattle drives. Sometimes we took two days, camping out the first night; sometimes, if the weather was cool enough, we could make the drive in one. Once, when there was an overnight stay and one drover, our hired man, stayed with the herd, I was shone why buffalo chips made such good fuel in times gone by: dried cow chips worked exactly the same way, burning with a hot, blue flame. Actually, dry chips are just compressed grass. If I remember right, our cowboy hired man heated a can of beans over the fire.

I was nine when I first did a one-day drive, riding and walking my mare, Spark Plug, the thirty-five miles. I still feel painfully tired whenever I think of it, riding back from the hills at night in the narrow truck cab between two men, my father and our hired man, Eldon Garski. I had never been so tired. It was a memorable trip though: it was so cold and windy we walked part of the time to keep warm, leading the horses; it drizzled a little; and Garski's mare pitched with him, having got weeds under her tail. We made the long drive without so much a losing an animal. Actually, we never lost an animal during a drive. It was my Grandpa Fred who always killed a couple of animals, driving too hard and never making allowances for the weather. My father remarked about it, always with a thoroughly disgusted head shake. *The Old Man is no cattleman,* he would say. Grandpa's herding methods only confirmed my early opinions of him, which I had formed long before I was nine.

"Sparky," which is what I called Spark Plug, was my full-time mount, being left in the barn with the saddle on and cinch loose because I was too small to saddle her. When I needed to ride, for work or fun, I tightened the cinch and bridled her. She could not be tied, and didn't ground tie (that is, stay put when you dropped the reins to the ground) very well either, so when I was with Sparky I had to stay with her. Garski, our lanky Burwell cowboy who became like one of the family, said Sparky was a mustang and thought he could break her to being tied, but all he did was prove she was more stubborn than he was. He tried tying her in a stall and putting a chain behind her, but all it did was frighten her, and he gave it up. I watched the process and thought it needlessly cruel, though it certainly would have been nice to have been able to tie her. She had other peculiarities too, trying to get too close to fence posts if I rode her on a lope or gallop through a turn. I sometimes had to take a leg out of a stirrup to keep it from being knocked against a post. She pitched with me once, in a cornfield, but the closest I ever came to being thrown was once when she shied at a snake. I was too small to use the actual stirrups, but I was able to use the straps that held them. Sparky and I herded cows, delivered water to hay and threshing crews, rode around town, especially on rodeo days, and played cowboys and Indians on horseback. A couple of our granaries were converted boxcars, which fit perfectly with the western movies we saw with Hop-a-long Cassidy and the other heroes of the black and white screen. Some of the players would climb the boxcar while Sparky and I and a neighbor horseman would tear by, cap guns blazing. The poor mare worked up quite a lather some days.

It was at the age of nine that I begin driving the stacker team. The hay stacker we used was the high lift kind: the sweeper operator shoved the hay onto the stacker's lifting platform, and the team pulled a cable that lifted the hay and threw it backward to make a stack. Someone with a pitchfork stayed on the stack and arranged the hay as with progressive loads it got higher and higher. At a certain point the team driver had to remove and replace bolts in the mechanism to lift the hay higher. The problem was that the horses had got used to going only so far, and when the bolts were changed they had to go farther—if they didn't, the hay fell down into the mechanism and the driver of the stacker team had to get a pitchfork and clean it out, and then somehow get the team to move the extra distance to lift the hay. If the horses went too far, they could throw the load of hay off the back of the stack, or dump the hay on top of the person on the stack doing the stacking. The stacker had to be pretty agile anyway, jumping around on the bouncy hay to arrange it and avoiding being hit by the load; and things could really get interesting for him when, rarely, the load of hay included a rattlesnake.

Putting up the hay was done at the hottest, driest, dustiest time of the year. With that and trying to make those horses go where I needed them to go and stop where I needed them to stop, I sometimes ended the day with a severe headache. I did not ask if the responsibility was too much for a nine year old, and I don't think it was. I had headaches off and on for years and was treated for sinus problems that were thought to be the cause by doctors who even had me sniffing penicillin treated air and getting penicillin shots. Penicillin was the new miracle drug then, and doctors tried it on anything. It had no effect on sinus problems—or headaches. In my late teens they mostly went away. I don't remember if the headaches became fewer when we replaced the stacker team with a truck. The cable was attached to the truck's front end, and I simply had to back it up to lift the load. I could see what was happening better—you drove the stacker team with your back to the load—and I could stop exactly as I wanted. To me the truck was a vast improvement, a kind of predictor of a time when we all learned it was easier to check the cattle with a pickup than a horse—not as romantic, perhaps, but easier. Before we started using the truck, I had learned to pick up a pitchfork and show it to the horses when I changed the bolts. After the first few instances of getting their rears poked and farting loudly in surprise and indignation as they jumped ahead, seeing the pitchfork was all they needed.

In the first years on that farm horses were still in use on the rake at haying time, but the sweep was always powered by tractor then. I have vague memories of sweeps being horse driven too, probably in my Grandpa Mike's hayfields before our move to the Sutherland place. My father liked horses and liked to work them and still did some of the cultivating with them. We had two teams then: the bays Bill and Bob and the dapple grays, Dutch and Esther. Horses required a lot of attention, feeding, harnessing, cooling off, grooming. Their feet had to be trimmed, whether shod or not. We didn't shoe them then that I can remember, having no rocks or other hard walking to contend with. Horses had to be protected from flies and disease. When they were brought in from the fields after a day's work, their needs had to be met before your own. All these things were essential parts of my growing up. What is amazing to me is that my growing up happened just as all this was being changed by engine powered machinery. Of course, I thought nothing of it then, except that the truck made life easier when stacking hay; but looking back I see how fortunate I was to be part of a world fast disappearing. It didn't happen all at once: we were still using horses on the fourth farm, and by then I had learned about hames and collars, feed bags, fly nets, and tugs—but draft horses were not around much longer for us, after we left the Sutherland place. We always had saddle horses, though, as we always had cattle, but with pickups and trucks and squeeze chutes available we used them less and less. My father's interest in horses never ceased; horses were something he knew about.

At threshing time Sparky and I carried jugs of water to the threshing crews. I would tie a jug to the saddle horn and we would walk or canter as the need for water by the different workers seemed to require. The jugs were wrapped in burlap and soaked so that evaporation would keep the water cool. The evaporative canvass bag was not around yet. We had the loaders, the unloaders, and the operators to consider. I tried to keep up, but I soon discovered that walking the mare was better than any other gait. When Sparky trotted or cantered the jug bounced against my leg. After a little of this the process became painful, with bruises at the end of the day. But it was important work. It also meant I would spend a good deal of time on horseback. My straw hat always had to have a tie down, which meant that at anything faster than a walk, the cord, usually a shoestring, was around my neck and the hat was riding on my back. Overalls were standard before jeans became common gear, but I think I had cowboy boots from about age seven on. Western wear had not yet assumed universal popularity. Garski, from the Burwell ranch country, did fill the cowboy image, even rolling his own from the Bull Durham tie sack—but then my father did that. Cowboy attire was a coming thing though, probably because of the movies more than anything else. Most of our toy guns took the shape of Colt's pistols, but we had Dick Tracy types as well. We had rubber-band guns too. You cut the pistol profile from wood, mounted a clothespin on the handle, and stretched a piece of inner tube from the muzzle to the clothespin. Squeezing the handle fired the band. The longer the barrel, the tighter the stretch, the more the velocity. Boys could have shootouts with such weapons—and did. You could also shoot down paper targets and harass flies.

Except for some of the machine work, like ditching so that the field could be irrigated, sugar beets required hand labor, and that's what the Mexican family provided. The family did work as a family, all able bodied members participating. First came the thinning. When the beets were planted the seed was simply sewn in rows, and the beets came up too thick to attain any size. So they had to be thinned. This was done with a hoe, workers chopping out spaces to let the better plants grow. After thinning came weeding, which happened several times over the summer as the beets grew. Irrigating lasted day and night for periods of time, depending upon precipitation, which could be pretty sparse in our part of the world.

Finally, there came piling and topping, part of the harvest; and harvest happened only after a good freeze in the fall. The beets were pulled from the ground by machine, and then each beet was picked up individually with the long curved pick on the end of the beet knife and the leaves cut off (topped) and the topped beet was thrown in a pile. The pile was picked up, by hand in those days, the loader using a beet fork, and loaded into a truck. This was all hand work, back-breaking hard work. I know, because my brother and I earned our bicycles that way one fall. In fact, I know first hand the whole routine, except for the actual loading the beets: I would not have been able to do that at the time. Dad gave us a couple acres of beets as our own, so long as we did the work: thinning, weeding, topping, piling. Piling at harvest time was the worst, although weeding in the hot summer sun was not exactly fun. Topping was the most enjoyable part because you got to use a beet knife and whack the tops off. We missed school to harvest our beets and were rewarded with green and red Schwinns. I had already learned to ride on a bike belonging to a young man who came out to help with the farm work, or work around the yard occasionally. He was fourteen and diabetic and had to go home during the day at times. At first, I was too small to mount the bike but discovered that if I placed the bike near a stump I could get on the stump and push off.

We almost always had a young man who did odd jobs as well as a hired girl to help in the house. Most of our "hired help" were like members of the family, but sometimes things didn't work out. One young man, a kind of shirttail relative, became an impossible irritant, to me anyway; and one needy hired girl turned out to be a pathological liar; but I think it was from that farm that one of the hired girls eventually became an aunt.

My father was a very good beet farmer. I have a sterling silver watch fob given to him by the beet company that says, *High-ten Grower, awarded for highest beet production, Ovid* (where the plant was), *1941.* The obverse is engraved, *Chris Reitz.* The fob is elaborate: it pictures a large sugar beet over a field with a farmer on a tractor and a sugar factory, which is what we called a beet processing plant, in the background.

If it rained too much for field work, Dad took us fishing at Sutherland Reservoir. In the earlier years we dug worms and tied cane poles on top of the Plymouth. Later we had real rods and reels. You could buy a reel for a quarter then. And sometimes, after checking the cattle in the sandhills, we would fish the sandhill lakes for bullheads and perch. Some of our sandhill excursions included uncles, aunts, and cousins too, and one summer we all got together for a real fishing trip to Minnesota.

Dad nailed a barrel hoop above the garage door so we could shoot hoops, though the court was dirt and gravel, as was the garage floor. It seems a little strange now to think that we had a garage when the toilet was a privy outside, and a pitcher pump supplied water inside the house. We had electricity, which I remember so vividly because when lightning hit the house during one of summer thunderstorms the charge came through the wiring, destroying a mixer, and hitting Garski, who had his bedroom in the house and lived with us, in the shoulder. A kind of luminescent blue ball floated around the living room briefly. Garski's shoulder hurt him for a long time. It always seemed to me that summer thunderstorms did mostly harm: not only were they frightening with high wind and slashing rain, but they always were wild with thunder and lightning and often brought hail. The hard rain washed gullies in our carefully ditched fields too. The one good thing about thunderstorms was that if they made the fields muddy enough we got to go fishing. The wet ground made it easier to dig for worms too.

Sutherland itself was within walking distance—or roller-skating distance, if you carried your skates to the sidewalks. I could roller skate to school if I used the rough highway too until I got to the town's sidewalks; but actually skating the highway was not enjoyable and not very fast because of its rough surface, so I usually carried the skates until I got to the sidewalks. My skates seemed pretty fancy to me: the clamps that held the skates to my shoes and were tightened with a special key were shaped like the wings on the god Mercury's feet that you see in pictures. The sidewalks were often broken by the roots of the big trees, for the yards were large even where the houses weren't, and the citizens of small towns then still cultivated trees and lawns between the sidewalks and the street. You learned to miss the big cracks with short or long strokes and to jump the uneven edges. The skates were essential at recess or noon lunchtime when everyone gathered on the huge paved area at the school's entrance to skate and to do spins. Even after we got our bicycles and rode them to school we took our skates.

As important as the skates were marbles, another recess and after school challenge, and challenge it was; for the winner kept the marbles he won. I wish I could remember the names of all the marbles games we played. A favorite was called "holies," I think. Contestants dug a small hole into which each contributed, and from a set distance each "lagged" to get his lagging marble in the hole to win the marbles. Another game was "fish pot" where each contestant placed marbles inside a fish-like shape drawn in the dirt and shot at them until he missed. You had to knock the object marble out of the pot to claim it and could keep shooting until you missed. Another game was "bull ring." You drew a large circle, put your marbles in the middle and took turns shooting from outside. You had to knock the marble out to claim it. Everyone had his favorite "shooters" and "steelies." The steelies were used to lag during "holies" mostly, but could be shooters too. Girls didn't play marbles. When I finished the marble stage I had over four hundred marbles of all kinds in an old cotton purse. I lost track of them, but they turned up in my mother's house when we got ready to sell everything after it became obvious she would reside in a North Platte care facility. A collector bought them for the "collectibles," and the money went into the pot for mother's care.

We played mumblety peg too. Every boy had a pocket knife. I can recall a whole series of fine pocket knives of different sizes that I had then, some with red, some with yellow handles, all curved beautifully to fit your hand. Pocket knives were an absolute necessity: you needed them to make the grooves in slingshot crotches that held the rubber bands; you needed them when you went fishing; you needed them in kite making and maintenance and a million other things like showing off the pretty red or yellow handles.

In Sutherland, we had a gym class, but dodge ball and occasional soccer are all I remember. I remember the soccer because I can recall a game in which I scored two goals and the dodge ball because I played basketball in the same gym later when I was in high school in Paxton. Sometimes we called it "smash mouth." I was good at dodge ball and enjoyed it immensely Another noon and recess activity was football, with every boy available playing, meaning large numbers on each side—and it wasn't touch football either: tackling and piling on was part of the fun. All the boys, whether third-graders or eighth-graders played, and I remember it mainly because a friend of mine was a good tackler, and because during one game I intercepted a pass and ran for a touchdown before the bigger boys could catch me. (One has to remember all one's triumphs, no matter how insignificant; there seem to be so few.)

My memories of school in Sutherland include some disappointments—though occurring long ago, during the last half of the third grade through the first half of the sixth (my brief tenure there), never forgotten. There was the all-school athletic day of races during which one judge declared me the winner while another judge declared his nephew the winner. The nephew got the flashlight, and I felt outrage for a long time. There were the fights I had defending my brother, who was small for his age, and having to soak my hands in Epsom salts to get the swelling down. There were the two bullies I cowed and the one I didn't. Most of all was the disappointment of not being skipped a grade: I was already attending the fourth grade class and doing the work when the modern educators of the day decided, as I was the youngest in the third grade class, that my "socialization" would be forever damaged if I didn't continue in third grade. I have always remembered that word—"socialization." It seemed utterly stupid to me then and does still, suggesting as it does, making you something my Grandpa Fred would have called a Bolshevik. My mother had graduated at sixteen, which I knew, and began college at sixteen, with no apparent damage I could see. This cost me a year all through life, a year that might well have changed my profession (because the Korean War intervened in my plans, something I did not know then, of course); but I did know that it was utterly stupid even then, resented it, and hope I was something of a pain to the third grade teacher, Miss Conroy, who for the way she blustered around the room I called "Convoy." There was that incident at the pencil sharpener too—is it not strange how well we remember injustices?

As important as school was it could never compete with being part of a crops and cattle operation. I remember milking half a cow at a time in below zero temperatures when my father was too ill to get out of bed. It was too cold for me to milk the whole cow, so I would milk half, go in to warm myself, then go out and do another half. This took a long time, as I think we were milking four cows then. But I did it all: cows had to be milked, twice a day. I was seven or eight years old.

It was during these years that my mother introduced me to the Carnegie Library in town. I can't remember everything I read, but I know I read all the Nancy Drew and "Buddy" books there on the summer days when I wasn't carrying water on Sparky, haying, or swatting flies for a penny a piece in the pump house. We all had to work in the garden too, weeding or picking. The garden produced many bushels in excess of what we ourselves could use, not only more than we could use immediately, but more than we needed to can also. Peas were especially abundant. We finally resorted to shelling them with the wringer on the clothes washer. We sold the excess to the townspeople. There was a lawn to mow, hard work for an eight or nine year old with a push mower, but sometimes the hired boy did it.

About a week after I turned ten the Japanese attacked Pearl Harbor, and the world was turned, if not upside down, at least very strange, even for a ten year old. When the Oklahoma went down it took distant cousins with it who were always identified to us as "the Blitz twins." The attack seemed especially strange because we had known Japanese persons as neighbors to Grandpa Fred and proprietors of our favorite restaurant in North Platte for as long as we knew anything. Grandpa's neighbors were friends and fine farmers who shared their excellent watermelons and sweet corn. I had never heard anything but good about the Matsitanis, anything but respect for their ability as farmers. To my knowledge the war caused them no special trouble in our world, as they maintained their places in the community, at least so far as I knew.

The draft had a drastic effect. Although my father did not have to go into the service because of his family, age, and essential occupation, we lost Garski to the army. After his initial training he showed up in uniform and demonstrated rifle drill. My uncles Fred and Harry were drafted. Uncle Pete, who worked for a railroad was not. We found ourselves, quite suddenly, unable to get reliable help. I can remember one potential hired man who turned out to be a hopeless alcoholic. The Mexican family was there only in summer. I don't really know whether the draft affected them too. We had to deal with the rationing of fuel though it was essential to our operation. We were restricted to thirty-five miles an hour when we had to take our Plymouth to get repairs for the machinery—or go to the dentist, and we had to make certain, when we wore out or blew out a tire on our equipment, that the hole in the tire was big enough to justify a new tire—though obviously any hole, especially in the tires of that time, made any tire used for heavy equipment useless. The government had taken it upon itself to decide exactly how big a hole in a tire had to be, so sometimes we had to help a little. Parts for the machinery were sometimes in short supply.

Some of the trains going by, so near our house, began carrying khaki clad young men, who could be seen in the windows and who sometimes waved as they went rapidly by. Sometimes flatcars had exotic olive-colored trucks and tanks. We no longer had men off the trains knocking at the back door and asking for sandwiches. Olive colored military convoys passed on the Lincoln Highway.

The radio had nothing but war news, anxious even for a ten year old, and I listened whenever I could, hoping for good news. It seems to me that I listened to the radio for hours at a time, hoping to hear that the war had stopped. But it never stopped, not while we were on the Sutherland place. Sutherland, small town in the middle of a continent, practiced blackouts and drills. We participated in everything as patriotically as we could. It was years later that we learned that we were being imposed upon by a paternalistic government that did not trust its citizens to take the war with sufficient seriousness. Shortages, at least in part, were an unnecessary imposition, and that realization did nothing but increase our very American cynicism toward government in general, though Uncle Roger had been helped at a critical time (back in the days of the Lone Tree Ranch) by a job with the depression's WPA. The story, which he liked to tell over our occasional family games of Pinochle, was that he could have a job operating heavy equipment if he demonstrated that he could run a Caterpillar. He had handled lots of equipment but not that particular machine; but as the story goes, he climbed aboard and faked it long enough to figure it out and land the job. The story always ended with a grin and a chuckle. Apparently, during his WPA experience, he had a hand in creating the irrigation system in the north valley.

My personal acute shortage caused by the big war was airplane glue. I was in the model airplane construction stage of my life; glue was essential, but it took many trips to the local drug store to maintain a supply. Sometimes construction was impossible for weeks. During the big war, even a ten year old was made to feel the pinch, personally. During my model airplane shutdowns I did woodburning. Woodburning required only the woodburning kit I found at the hardware store and electricity.

At that time of my life I felt the pinch in more direct ways, for I frequently had a lot of pain, other than the headaches. I had terrible pains in my legs and in my side at times. It was not, apparently, appendicitis, for we were aware of that, my brother Mike having his removed when he was only seven. Eventually, the pains went away, except the headaches, which I had periodically for years.

I never saw our important tall, lanky, hired man, Eldon Garski, again. He visited my parents a couple of times after the war, driving a red convertible and wearing a big white Stetson, they said, on his way to manage a dude ranch in Montana or someplace. He had been on Omaha Beach and had won silver and bronze stars, several times, according to their report.

There came a March, before the war ended, when we became "southsiders," moving from the irrigated South Platte valley to the dry land south of Paxton. Sparky and the Morgan horse that tried to kill my father were gone by then, the Morgan to a rancher who liked to race him—he was very fast—but the horse nearly killed one of his cowboys, impaling him on a saddle horn.

It took a number of truck loads to move our stuff: machinery, cattle, household goods. The new house, until we had it enlarged, was much too small for us and our belongings. I had, for some reason, burned all my models before the move, including a Messerschmidt, except one, a glider I had not completed that had a seven-foot wing span. My model airplane collection burned just like the real airplanes we saw in the movies. I remember putting the wings and fuselage of the glider, along with other things, on the buffet in the new house, until it was safe to move them elsewhere. Eventually I was able to put the glider together, but

I never did get its weight and balance right. Later, I would build more model airplanes, but my life, our lives, had apparently entered a new phase.

Lone Tree Ranch

The second place we lived on was in the north valley, the land stretching from the between-the-rivers hills to the North Platte River. It was a large place, with a big pasture and extensive farm land. The house was located in the pasture section. Part of the house, which was located near the top of a rather steep hill, was constructed of concrete, and the concrete part was inside the hill. A concrete water cistern was a little above that. We had running water there, and electricity, but no indoor toilet until my father built one in the part of the house that was built into the hill. That part of the house was always dark and cool, especially in summer.

The hill was steep enough to coast a tricycle down, and the barn was below the hill too. There were pigeons in the barn. A cob pile was near by, and one of my jobs was to load cobs into a wagon with wooden sides and pull it up the hill to burn in the kitchen stove. It was hard, dirty work, handling the man-sized cob fork to load the wagon and get it up the hill, but you could get into the wagon and coast down the hill, holding the handle backward and steering. Getting down upright wasn't a sure thing, however. Tippy as it was, the trike was more dependable, especially if you held your feet out wide, like outriggers.

I was only five or six years old when we moved to this combination farm-ranch. My mother named it the Lone Tree Ranch because it had only one tree near the yard. I don't remember exactly where the tree was. On the winding dirt road to the farm land was a large grove of trees, important because there Dad cut for me the makings of my first sling shot. I remember it took a lot of reminding to get the tree crotch that forms the basis of a slingshot. Inner tubes of the time were made of real rubber and worked perfectly when tied to the matching arms of the tree crotch "Y"; the pouch that held the stone to be shot was always made of leather cut from the tongue of a discarded shoe. The Lone Tree Ranch slingshot became the first of generations of this indispensable boy-tool. Years later, when we returned to the area just to see it again a herd of mule deer occupied the grove, but there were no deer when we lived there.

We lived there before the North Platte was dammed by Kingsley Dam. We were actually able to watch the dam being built on some of our Sunday excursions west to Ogallala; but when we moved to the place no trees lined the river and delineated its course as they would after the dam was built, for the river flooded every year and washed everything out except for a few willows. Nowadays, with all the cottonwoods and Russian olives lining the river, along with the extensive stands of willows, few would realize how the Platte was before the dams. The old mile wide and foot deep description is found only in old diaries, and some old histories. The riparian area is still changing, with the Russian olives taking over, cottonwoods becoming fewer and fewer.

My father did a lot of trapping when we lived on this place. In winter he would have a shed lined with stretched muskrat pelts. He trapped beavers from the river and especially from the irrigation canal, where the beavers were digging burrows and doing a lot of damage to the canal's banks. He had to get a special permit to trap there, but the ditch company was happy to have someone catch the beavers. Their pelts were valuable. Also valuable were skunk pelts; and I remember very distinctly being in Dad's shed while he skinned a skunk. He trapped coyotes and badgers too, and said that they were harder to trap than the muskrats or beavers, especially the coyotes.

On the farm part of the place my brother and I discovered an old unpainted house. A couple of windows were intact, so having never had a chance to break a window before, we threw a couple of rocks to the very satisfying sound of breaking glass only to learn later that this was the "beet house" for the Mexican family my father would eventually hire. Dad was not pleased, but he did nothing but shake his head and explain to us that the house would actually be used after it was fixed up. The first thing he had to do was remove part of an outside wall and eliminate the huge bee colony that lived there. He borrowed a smoking machine—it looked like a coffee pot—smoked the bees and removed the hive, which filled several tubs with wax and honey. I remember being surprised at how brown everything was, not yellow, the way you expect honey to be. My parents melted the wax and put the honey in jars. This was exactly the kind of new adventure I always associated with my father: he would learn anything to do anything it seemed to me. Later, on the Sutherland place, he had actually used sheep to clean up an overgrown hog lot. We had never had sheep before, or even seen many of them; and my father, as a cattleman, belonged to a group that normally hand nothing good to say about sheep. But he not only used the sheep to clean up the lot, which they did quickly and efficiently, but he bought a pair of used hand shears and sheared them. I remember especially how dusty and oily the wool was. Then he sold the wool and the sheep, and we never had sheep again.

Our nearest neighbors, on the north side of the dirt road that led to town, were the Sadles, who were still there years later; but on the south side for a time were my Uncle Roger and his family. We visited back and forth a good deal. What I remember most was their coal fired stove that was especially warm in winter and their bringing Dad back home one evening, when he had an accident with the Plymouth. I do not know what caused the accident or in which direction he was going at the time, but it happened on the road to town. I know it didn't permanently ruin the Plymouth because it was the car Dad drove at seventy miles an hour to the Sutherland hospital with me when I got my foot caught under a flywheel shaft. My cousin from down the road and I had been playing around a piece of Sadle's equipment when my foot got in the wrong place. The foot was not crushed, but it swelled hugely, and I had to hop around on one foot for quite awhile.

We seemed to have a lot of fence to fix on that place, and I often went with my dad in the horse drawn wagon he used for fence posts and wire. The steel clad wagon wheels made a grinding sound on parts of the road or were completely quiet in the sandy or dusty parts of the track, the horses switching their tails and occasionally shaking their manes against the flies. It was always a pretty leisurely and quiet time. I generally sat on the open tailgate with my legs hanging over while Dad sat in the seat and handled the horses. One day I fired my cap gun; the horses jumped and left me sitting in the road. My father generally just shook his head at youthful experiments; but he found this one particularly funny, and I felt particularly foolish. Probably the best discipline for boys growing up in my circumstances was the fear of being embarrassed before men, though in my case my mother always said I was born old and reasonable.

I should have been embarrassed when I crowed for my (I think) first grade teacher who was invited to "supper" one evening. We had been, for some reason, making animal sounds in class, so when asked to make mine I crowed to the hills. Roosters flapped their wings before crowing, and I did that too. If it didn't embarrass me then, it does now, thinking about it. Maybe my mother was right.

My first direct experience with gardens was on this place. The garden was down the road, below the big irrigation ditch, near the beet house. What I remember most are tomatoes, nice red tomatoes, summer heat, flies, and mosquitoes. I don't remember what I was supposed to do. I do remember how much more pleasant summer afternoons were, lying on the cool floor in the house listening to Mother's regular radio program, something called "Ma Perkins." Ma certainly had her problems. I think another soap was "Portia's Life," or something like that. Sharing the floor with me would have been Wonkie Poo, our cat.

This was the only cat we ever had in the house, though on some of our places we had a dozen or more outside and in the barns. Wonkie Poo played with us regularly. She was orange and striped and not very big. She was always especially interested in feet, especially bare feet.

At some point at the Lone Tree Ranch I was allowed to fire father's .22 Remington for the first time, only with his direct supervision, of course. I was allowed to ride with the men, my father and some of my many uncles, in the car while they looked for pheasants in the fall. I received a B-B gun for my sixth birthday. It was equipped with a long peep sight that looked like a telescopic sight but wasn't. In order to cock it I had to put the butt-stock under one leg to get enough purchase on the cocking lever. I stalked the barn pigeons and sparrows with the B-B gun without much success. It wasn't very powerful; if the light was right you could see the B-B leave the barrel. But it was an important possession for a boy too young yet for a .22.

I can remember only one time when we tried to go fishing. It was Sunday; so we went with Uncle Roger's family, but the roads were very muddy, and we were lucky to get turned around and get back home. We had to push the car in the mud. It was an unpleasant, disappointing, dirty trip, but the juniper trees along the road—which we called cedars—were a novelty. The entire hillside above the narrow road was covered with junipers. Trees of any kind were a novelty in our country then. You could drive thirty miles in the sandhills and never see one. There was our grove toward the road to town, and Sadles had mulberry trees. Grandpa Fred had big trees around his yard. But except around some farm yards the country was mainly treeless—stoneless too. Finding slingshot fodder meant picking from gravel on the road.

During the school year the vehicle that took me to school in town was a car driven by one of the parents of a classmate who lived in town. The other passengers were the sons and daughters of Grandpa Fred's beet family, headed by Little Joe Gonzales. They eventually disappeared until the next beet season. My memories of those times are pretty limited: I remember experimenting with the marbles I had in my back pocket while in second grade. I slid down in my desk so that the marbles came out and rolled on the floor—and the teacher really did pick them up and put them in the fish bowl. I had been warned that she might do that, but sometimes one has to test things. I remember vividly how competent as artists were the Mexican kids I rode to school with when the teacher had us draw and color our drawings. She covered the blackboard with paper and let us draw on that large surface. *That's because they're older,* I was told by someone; *they don't get to go to school regularly.* They didn't seem any older to me, just better artists. Their horses really looked like horses. Another art class allowed us to color designs we made very heavily with vibrant colors juxtaposed, like purple and yellow or purple and blue. Novelty is easily remembered I guess.

I remember learning grammar and multiplication in that part of the third grade I attended before we moved to the Sutherland Place. We had contests at the blackboard to see who could do the multiplication tables fastest. I remember a cute red-headed third-grader name Helen Bersler. Years later when I returned to Paxton for high school, other members of my third grade class, who had remained in town during those years, remembered her too. We all wondered what happened to Helen Bersler. I also remember clearly how impatient I became with third-graders who couldn't seem to do something as simple as grammar and multiplication tables, especially grammar, and when I got to the third grade in Sutherland after our March move, remember the same impatience with the third-graders there.

One second grade recess activity that is vivid in memory is stick hockey. We played it with any hockey shaped stick we could find and a Carnation milk can. The can was soon smashed beyond recognition. I remember the hockey because I got a stick cut just above the right eye. Fortunately, the town had a doctor then, who was just across the street, and who stopped the bleeding. We also had "sword fights." We made our swords from lath, the guard too, which was an S-shaped piece of lath we cut a rectangular hole in to slip over the handle. The Mexican kids made the most graceful swords and had the most authentic and graceful moves. We broke a lot of swords. It didn't take long to take out the pocket knife and make a new one.

We also played something called "pom-pom pull-away," but the name is about all I remember about that game. It had something to do with running and drawing a line in the dirt. We played a lot of tag. There was a slide and teeter-totters. Helen Bersler liked to hang out around the slide and teeter-totters.

Probably the most exciting school event then was fire drill, especially if we had to go down the escape tube, which third-graders did. It was more fun if you were not the first to go, for not only did the tube get slicker and therefore quicker, but also you avoided the puddle of water that was always in the little hollow at the end of the tube. An important side-benefit was that everyone got to go outside for awhile. Being outside during a regular school day was a strange and wonderful thing. For one thing your weren't sitting. It always seemed to me that in school you sat a lot.

Sometimes, some government program, dealing with surpluses I suppose, delivered big boxes of apples to the school, and we were each given two of the biggest, prettiest, most delicious apples I had ever seen. The only problem was we had to eat them then and there, and they were just too big for one sitting, which ruined some of the enjoyment along with the novelty. All of our school needs were supplied by the school in those days, even the pencils. There is nothing like the smell of pencil-sharpener cedar to evoke visions of the big, red-bricked building—cedar and the box-elder bugs of spring. The box-elder bugs would swarm on the warm side of the school house where there was some kind of utility entrance—maybe for coal—covered with tar paper and tar. The smell of tar was always associated with spring and box-elder bugs.

In springtime we played baseball in the lot across the street, real baseball, not the softball stuff of later gym classes. This was a noontime activity, after we had emptied our lunch pails of their peanut butter and jelly sandwiches. The sandwiches were good by then, all soft and soggy, and what they left on our hands was probably what gave the baseballs their special color. I can't remember if we had any baseball gloves; I don't think so. The lot was sandy though, just like the stories or Norman Rockwell magazine covers.

I don't remember any cattle drives from the Lone Tree Ranch. Apparently we had enough pasture there. We also had hay fields, though I was too young then to participate directly. There was some talk of buying the place, which was up for sale for $13,000, a sum I remember very distinctly, a paltry sum now but not in those days when a double-dip cone with a cherry on top cost a nickel, and a fancy new Plymouth cost $800. Grandma Molly would apparently help finance the purchase if asked, but my father would not ask—remarks in later years suggested he wasn't interested in being obligated to family, especially his mother-in-law, who never forgot a favor she did you and never let you forget it either. Shortly after our tenure Grandma helped Uncle Andy buy a farm near Bayard. From that time on Uncle Andy always owned a farm. As a boy whose ears were always full of farm and finance talk, I was as puzzled then as now about the reluctance to find $13,000 for a place that seemed ideal for all of us.

The only other memories of a social life on the Lone Tree Ranch concern local dances, square dances I suppose, since even my childish hand was taken so that I would participate. These happened in a little, white building, which must have been a school house in another district. And there was an evening when a large gathering of neighbors and relatives showed up to involve my parents in a "shivaree," (charivari) a custom of the times which generally made newly-weds uncomfortable enough to feel like members of the community. I can't remember why my parents were involved, for it was too long after their marriage to have been for them.

I remember the land though; somehow I always seem to remember the land, the sandhills near the house and the hill the house was on; the road down the hill past the barn, turning toward the grove and fields below; the smell of dust and horses and hay. I seem to remember an irrigation canal between the beet house and the fields and a series of pipes used to siphon water from the laterals to the ditches in the fields and the canvas dams my father made to direct the water. My father seemed always to be wearing a pair of rubber boots with the tops turned down and carrying a muddy shovel. He would whistle softly to himself sometimes.

First Farm

I spent long Sunday afternoons on the porch that surrounded Grandpa Mike and Grandma Molly's house, listening to my father and the other men pitching horseshoes in the lane between the house and the large barn that looked as if it were made of carved stone blocks and had the Lute name and a date carved above the main barn entrance. You could hear the men talking and laughing and the clank of the horseshoes when they hit the steel peg. One Sunday they saddled a horse and marked off a distance and one of the men took off his boots and in his stocking feet raced the horse over the distance to see which, horse or man, was faster in the short run. I don't remember who won. On another Sunday I found a collection of tubes in Grandpa and Grandma's attic that turned out to be rolls of music for an old Victrola that was up there too. A narrow stairway led to the attic, which was hot and dusty. The Victrola could be wound up still and played distant and mournful sounds. My brother Mike had been born in Grandpa Mike's house.

Mrs. Lute, for whose family the barn had been built and named, and I celebrated our birthdays together from the time I was four. We had tea and cookies with a tiny, child's tea set she had. One year she presented me a wonderful, red toy barn, complete with rubber farm animals. In later years I might get a book, and when Mr. Lute died we were given much of the library. Mrs. Lute moved to town and lived in a house with a wonderful sun room that was always full of sunlight and books. During the southsider years, her daughter Harriet became my high school English and Latin teacher and sponsor of the yearbook for which, one year, I did the artwork in pen and ink, only to see most of it lost by the publisher. We had to use a couple of the drawings that survived over and over—a compromise yet strangely vivid in memory, probably because it is one of those things related to home that comes somewhere near an end of a long string of connections that began near the beginning. For I was only four when these events began although, according to my parents my memory began even earlier, one bit of evidence being a scene I described for them that turned out to be from a movie they took me to when I was three. I can do better than that—I think; for this is hard to believe, even for me: I have a strange recollection of the time when I first understood speech, not a word at a time either—sentences. Maybe that's not possible; but that's the way I remember it. My mother and my aunts said that my first word was *pretty*. I would look at things, one after another, they said, and say *pretty*. They said I said the word about things that were pretty. This is something I do not remember.

My first memories of the first farm are of a small house, not far from the main road into the north valley, where I caught the yellow school bus for kindergarten, and I was four when I started kindergarten and could read very well by the end of that school year. I do not know if I could read anything before I started, but there must have been some reason I was allowed to start school at that age, for I missed the official starting age by three months. Anyway, I remember the house, both inside and out, and the windmill nearby with its barrel through which the well water flowed where I was sent to get the butter we kept in a sealed lard pail.

You entered the house through a porch. There was a rifle hanging on the wall to the left as you entered. At sometime in those early years in conversation between my father and my uncles I heard the rifle was a .22 Special, obsolete already when I first heard of it—at least that's what it sounded like, already a relic of some distant time I would somehow never know about. Perhaps it is in tiny bits of evidence that hint at things we can never be a part of that ignites our sense of time. Our light was from kerosene lamps. I never lighted one, but I started to once when I got home from school before my parents had returned from some place and it got dark. I had seen them do it, so I took off the shade and got the match going, but the lamp didn't light immediately. I was afraid of what might happen so blew out the match and went to bed as in the dark I did not know what else I could do. They were never late when I was alone again.

For a while I had a little terrier name Spot, but not long after he came to live with us he ran out on the road and was killed by a car. We didn't have another dog while we lived there, but we did have other animals, because I remember going to a barn in winter, when even with my buckle overshoes my feet got so cold I thought they would freeze. I don't know why I went out then. I remember how intensely my feet hurt. We had another shed, a garage maybe, that I remember because when I went fishing for the first time I caught a small carp, and my father loaded it with rat poison and threw it into that building. It was dark and had a dirt floor. In early fall my father would go to that building and bring out watermelons that had stored there in piles of oats. The watermelons were always wet inside, fresh, and cool.

During beet harvest time my father got up very early, even earlier than usual, in the dark. Warm in bed I could hear my mother and father talking and see the light under the door. This happened every morning for awhile, soft voices and the light under the door, long before I had to get up an catch the bus for kindergarten.

We had "flash cards" in kindergarten. The teacher would hold up the cards and you were supposed to say the words. After a few sessions of flash cards we were divided into Brownies and Fairies. I didn't take long to realize that the Brownies weren't very good at flash cards. We had to have a rug to lie on every afternoon for a little while. It seemed pretty silly, but then so did other things, like getting ready to sing something in a play about Peter Rabbit. When I didn't take my bunny part seriously enough I was made a pea, and was supposed to wear a pea costume and say or sing something. The night of the pea performance I had a cold and had to stay home anyway. I did not feel left out.

During coloring period once we were given a bear to color. During the color selection I made the mistake of identifying the bear's butt, in so many words, and had to spend time in the coat closet for the nasty word. The closet was behind some doors that pivoted open into the room. There was a gap under the doors and I could see the ankle of one of the girl Fairies or Brownies standing for a presentation of some kind. Grabbing the ankle meant more closet time, but it at least alleviated some of the strain of not even being able to name the parts of an animal every country boy was familiar with. I had one other little scrape with authority. I was not very big then, and one of the older boys kept trying to pick a fight at recess. Finally, one winter day when we were outside with our mittens on, I told him if he wanted to fight we would fight, grabbed him by the hair and smacked him in the nose. His nose bled all over the place. I got a mild bawling out, but he never bothered me again. These little episodes only serve to demonstrate the distortion memory can provide, for I was never confrontational unless provoked, always enjoyed school, and the only real "trouble" I ever got into, sorry to say, was kindergarten closet time.

All in all, kindergarten was all right as we had books to read and writing to do and even with closet time they had to give you outstanding on your report card, on everything that counted anyway. Some of the children in that kindergarten class have been friends ever since.

I don't know why we went into the sandhills then as it was before the time we had our own cattle, but I know we went, maybe to look after Grandpa Mike's cows or go fishing—don't know—but I know we went because every time we went I got car sick or had a tooth ache and sometimes both. I had a lot of toothaches. I had to go to the dentist, finally. He ran the drill with his foot. The experience was worse than a toothache. I suppose I got the headaches, and car sick too sometimes, because my father smoked then, and there was always smoke in the back seat. When they let my ride up front, I didn't get car sick; but I still had toothaches.

I don't suppose the trip to the dentist happened until it became absolutely necessary, for we never seemed to have any money. I knew that money was a scarce commodity even as a very young child. An orange was an unusual treat, though we never lacked food, for except of exotic things like oranges we raised it all ourselves, canning even the meat in the time before freezers. For Christmas one year I remember a pencil and an orange. Another Santa brought a toy wooden boat. I think it was that year I was surprised with the little, red wagon from Grandpa Fred and Grandma Katherine. I can remember being surprised on fourth of July morning to be awakened by my father's shooting off fireworks in the area between the house and the main road. It turned out that my father always found money for fireworks. In later years we always had sparklers, and he always had rockets to fire into the night sky. He would drive a pipe into the ground to stick the rocket's protruding wooden tail in while we stood at a safe distance behind him. I am certain he went out of his way to make certain we were never left out of what he considered an important celebration, though we all knew that rockets were the most expensive of the fireworks. We were led to believe that shooting off fireworks was a very American thing to do. One year, along with the fireworks at the first house, he fired his shotgun. The first time I saw my father pitch dimes in a carnival game I could hardly believe it, and it was a long time before I realized that he could really afford to spend a dollar on a punch board in Ole's saloon.

But the impecunious years did not last long, really, though money, or rather lack of it, never seemed to be a worn out topic. The years of the first farm were the years at the depth of the great depression: not one of my parents' generation ever forgot it; and neither have those of us who were born to it. By the time we got to the second place, The Lone Tree Ranch, Christmas brought games and candies and important clothing. Christmas could be used as a barometer of a year's financial success and the succession of improvement over the years it seems, in retrospect. But it was many years before my mother got the china cabinet she talked about: some piece of new machinery or some repair always seemed to take precedent.

Grandpa and Grandma's house was just down the road, walking distance. We spent a lot of time there. Grandpa had the first radio in the area and we would go there just to listen. My aunts, Esther and Lydia, mother's sisters, were there a lot too. I was ring-bearer at Aunt Lydia's wedding, complete with velvet short pants and ruffled shirt. I followed my aunts around the house and roughhoused with my uncles. Aunt Lydia was the most fun. She laughed a lot. She called me "Rumpy" because I followed her around. All the ladies played the piano and sang. Grandpa Mike played the violin. Dad played the harmonica. Sunday afternoons and evenings in the living room (I don't think it was ever called "the parlor"),which seemed never to be open any other time, were times of music and conversation

When I attended kindergarten my Grandma Molly and I studied our spelling together, using a heavy, manila sheet with the words on it. Grandma Molly was of course fluent in German and knew some Russian too, but she wanted her English to be more than adequate and spoke with little accent. She said she remembered swimming in the Volga when she was young. She was good with figures and could do math in her head very quickly. She was short and quick and was always after someone to empty the "slop pail," the in-house garbage can of the day. The slop went to the hogs, of course. Grandma Molly was too quick to be thoughtful sometimes. Once, when I didn't move fast enough going up the basement stairs, she swatted me, a four year old, with the poker she had in hand. Steel, it hurt beyond anything I had ever been subject too, even toothaches, and I never forgot it or completely forgave her for it, even though she took me, the first son, on bus trips to Colorado as company after Grandpa Mike died. My father made no secret of the fact that she sometimes irritated him exceedingly. In his opinion, she had too many opinions about his business, many of them critical. He never said much, even to my mother, at least when I was paying attention; but his polite reserve became obvious to me as I grew older.

Grandpa Mike was a big, gentle man everyone liked. He was over six feet tall with red hair and blue eyes, and freckles. I have only limited memory of him, but what I remember is vivid. When we first went to Grandpa Mike's farm I could not go beyond the fence around the house without being attacked by a huge rooster, huge to me anyway. I was under siege one day when Grandpa came up from the fields to see what was happening. He chased off the rooster and gave me a stick. With that stick the rooster and I had it out the next time I was in the yard. From then on I was free—so long as I had the stick or Grandpa was near by. I had my first horseback ride, behind my father, on a black horse at Grandpa Mike's farm. The ride was rough and pretty scary, and remembering it is helped by an old picture depicting the event. Other old pictures show children in overalls standing before unpainted houses, depression pictures certainly; but our houses all had paint on them. Maybe they were beet houses, which weren't always kept up.

Another vivid memory I have is of Grandpa Mike coming up from the fields with his striped overalls ripped down the front of both legs. The rips in his overalls seemed to follow the stripes. He was walking but bleeding profusely. He had been cleaning out a "tumble-bottom" plow when it tripped. The sharp blades cut him severely when they rolled over.

The last memory I have of Grandpa Mike was at his funeral. Everyone walked by the casket in those days. There he was gray and covered with powder, but the powder couldn't hide his freckles. The smell of powder and flowers attends the thought of funerals still.

What a child notices and can remember is probably underestimated considerably. I remember distinctly a dark, very early morning in our little house down the road when the almost inaudible murmurs of disbelief meant my Grandpa Mike was dead. He had died suddenly, perhaps in his sleep, of what they called a cerebral hemorrhage. He was forty-seven. Even I understood how Grandpa Mike's sudden, early, unexpected death changed almost everything, for all I had to do was listen.

Grandpa Mike had been in the process of arranging to buy the Lute place, the place he farmed in partnership with Mr. Lute. It was a large farm, with rich soil, hay fields, pasture and frontage on the North Platte River. Sugar beets and small grains, hay and pasture, ample "ditch rights" for irrigation, ready access to markets, two large homes and a house for the beet family, an ice house, a smoke house—all these things were part of the farm and in use when I was a boy. The ice house was filled each winter with ice cut from the river and preserved in straw. I remember the smoke house smells of curing bacon and ham. There were gooseberry bushes and cherry trees and during springtime you heard bobwhite quail whistle from the orchard. Sometimes the irrigation ditch behind the orchard still had water in it in winter, and when it froze you could skate from Grandpa Mike's housed to Grandpa Fred's house. My father built a wooden sled, put on skates, and pulled me down the canal to Grandpa Fred's house.

At Grandpa's death Grandma simply sold everything. My father bought the cattle. I don't know why he did not take over the place; perhaps he could buy the cattle but not capitalize the rest; perhaps he had already made arrangements to settle on the Lone Tree Ranch, which we did soon after Grandpa's operation ceased. Grandpa Mike's funeral is the last thing I remember of our life on the first farm.

Grandma left the farm and went to stay with relatives in Lincoln, and then she worked as a housekeeper in various houses. I don't know whether she had to or just needed company and something to do. Finally, she got a house of her own. That's when she took me with her on trips, trips to the Colorado mountains by bus to hot baths, flowing streams, and forests of pine trees, exotic places to a seven year old. The women at the baths talked and tatted and talked about tatting. I saw my first tennis match, between teenagers near a stream, where they sometimes knocked the balls over the fence into the mountain stream and had to chase the balls down the rushing water. I got a wooden hatchet and a birch-bark canoe and got to drink 7-Up every day. We were living on the Lone Tree Ranch during some of the Colorado adventures and on the Sutherland Place during others.

Then Grandma got married again to Mr. Hook and moved to Bayard. I visited them in Bayard every summer for a week, reading comic books and building model airplanes and eating the exotic bread and sausage from the German store downtown and going to the German-Lutheran church where much of the ceremony was in German. We were Southsiders by then.

Then Grandpa Hook died, and after awhile Grandma married Grandpa Shaffer and moved to Scottsbluff, into a house next door to another German-Lutheran church. I was too old for visits then, but my family made occasional trips to Scottsbluff, where we visited and bought German sausage since my father did not make it anymore; and we always bought a few "krautburgers" from Henry's Market, the only place such things were made. Sometimes Grandma Molly and Grandpa Shaffer would visit us at the fourth farm, and Grandpa Shaffer would show us his new fishing tackle and giver us each a quarter. Grandma and Grandpa would go crappie fishing and exceed the limit every chance they had. I was indignant that my Grandparents were what we called "game hogs" and German-Lutherans at the same time.

We did not go to Scottsbluff much, and when we were on our way to Yellowstone Park for a vacation and some fly fishing we started driving through town without stopping. My father said he had had enough of Grandma, who always thought vacations (except hers) a waste of time and money. But when we did stop Grandma had ice cream and kuchen. Grandpa raised pigeons and had a garden, and frequently a new, used Chevrolet.

On our first trips to Scottsbluff we played a game called "who can see Chimney Rock first," which brother Mike never won. That's how we discovered he needed glasses and had never seen Dad's whiskers. Little brother Tim and sister Rosalee practiced their special language on these trips. They had developed a special kind of whisper language only they could understand. It was a one hundred thirty mile trip one way. One of our just-after-the-war cars was a used Dodge that replaced the Plymouth the train wiped out. On a Scottsbluff trip the crankshaft failed and we had to have it hauled back on a truck. Our Uncle Andy, who had a farm near Bayard then, took us home.

Once, all three families, mine, Uncle Roger and Aunt Esther's, spent Christmas together in Uncle Andy and Aunt Lydia's Bayard house, a big house with an impressive wooden staircase. There were lots of cousins by then, especially Uncle Roger and Aunt Esther's. They eventually had eight children, seven surviving. We stayed overnight on that occasion as by then everyone lived a long way from everyone else. Eventually, Uncle Andy and Aunt Lydia moved from the Bayard farm back to the home country. For the rest of their lives the three families lived within thirty miles of each other. Our family spent the major portion of its social time with my mother's sisters and their husbands rather than my father's relatives. It was Lydia and Andy and Esther and Roger rather than John and Marie, Rae and Anna, Earl and Helen, or Pete and Emma. Pete and Emma lived far away, in Kansas City, so we saw them rarely anyway. The cousins I spent time with were Uncle Andy's and Uncle Roger's. Those closest in age were Uncle Andy and Aunt Lydia's daughter, Molly, named for her grandmother; and Uncle Roger and Aunt Esther's son, whom we always called Roddy, though he was really Roger, named for his father. The three couples relationships had been formed long before I was born, even before Lydia and Andy were married. Aunt Lydia was the first to die, of cancer.

Grandma Molly died, outliving two husbands; but Grandpa Shaffer lived several more years. Grandma Molly (Amalia) had talked of dying for years: every visit included such talk, which got to be a kind of special penalty for visiting. When she did finally die she was taken back to Paxton and buried beside Grandpa Mike. She left several houses and bank accounts to my mother and her surviving sister, so there were more trips to Scottsbluff and nearby Gering to settle accounts.

When Grandpa Shaffer died only his first wife was mentioned in his obituary, though he and Grandma Molly had been married twenty years. My family was suitably indignant at the not uncommon slight, but, of course, had little contact with that phase of Grandpa Shaffer's life anyway. Still it was remarked, and the Scottsbluff connection was permanently severed with a strange kind of finality as if negotiations in civility had been carried on unsuccessfully with a strange planet.

Home

In the end, of course, there is no way to make consistent a description of the sights, sounds, and smells that have become internalized as memory, for everything that has happened to create consciousness is infinitely interwoven. It is more than the simple interconnectedness that literary minds have decided to call stream of consciousness: it has to do with the connections between feeling and knowing, the past and the present and dreams of the future, especially dreams of what might be as well as what might have been. An objective stranger, set suddenly down in the midst of what is home to me, would wonder why anyone would give the place a second thought, a place of ordinary human beings living in an monotonous landscape that has never graced a calendar—hot in summer, cold in winter, windy most of the time. To the north the sandhills roll on endlessly; to the south large fields bordered by fences that always run with the cardinal points of the compass stretch on and on. The valleys of the Plattes are as flat as the name implies, making it easy to spot the water towers far before you come to the towns whose names are painted on them. Winters are long and mostly stark shades of brown, the trees along the rivers spiky and bleak, unless snow blows across the roads or blankets the countryside, relieving the bleakness with patterns—or adding to it.

Even summer green is short after the wheat turns golden, except in the irrigated fields. Yet those who live here notice quiet winter days and summers full of magpies flitting across the roads and through the trees along the river; and red-headed woodpeckers making staccato noises in the cottonwoods. Southsiders enjoy lark buntings soaring up and spiraling down over their prairie places in summer and meadowlark song, and the quiet voices of horned larks at snow time.

Most important to my memory are the quiet voices of my parents before dawn, when a beam of light under the bedroom door announces another hard day of manual labor or work with animals, the voices of my parents quiet and respectful between them; and though I cannot understand the words beyond the doorway, they are totally reassuring to a child, always. I hear a noisy family at dinner, my Aunt Lydia's laughter, bulls bellowing, the nicker of horses and the squeak of saddle leather, dry stalks rustling, and the loose rattle of grasshopper wings. I smell dust and cow's breath and dark newly plowed earth and newly dug potatoes and just-combined wheat and sausage frying. I see rippling heat waves over sandhill grass and hear the trilling call of sandhill cranes and the raucous crowing of rooster pheasants and see their tracks in patches of snow, and recognize neighbor's windmills and those water towers with small towns' names on them.

I remember that one of the first things we did when we became southsiders was to build a brooder house. It came as a kit with eight ready-built sides we bolted together to form an octagonal building that could be evenly heated for the four hundred tiny, yellow chicks that we would get each spring from cheeping cardboard boxes delivered to the railroad station. We furnished the house with a large, propane fired heater with a round steel top just high enough from the floor to accommodate the chicks—a large, artificial hen which would hover over the incessantly cheeping chicks for several weeks—we put chemicals against disease in the water jars before we tipped them over in the "waterers," made certain the mash used for food was dry and clean. Chicks that were timid or weak were given special attention—placed in cardboard boxes near the kitchen stove, cared for until they could fend for themselves without being picked on. The brooder house was a round, warm, noisy, secure place, just like our own—but when you opened the door to enter there was an immediate hush; the incessant cheeping din instantly stopped, as if a hawk had flown over; and for an instant that miniature world became as quiet as a cathedral. It was as if there were some sudden recognition that the warmth and companionship and care were merely some kind of truce with the way things are, that maturity brings only disaster, that somewhere even more profound than the paradox of being cared for to become food is the paradox of being the human doing the caring and the eating.

I have at times thought of the brooder house and wondered if it defines or exaggerates my sense of how things really are. We built it and it was a warm place full of noise and activity at a cold time, but for its inhabitants the future was as exquisitely brief as was our own there—to be commemorated and explained now only by the myth we call memory. Others have other myths, of course; but for me memory without any pretense of justification will have to suffice, for any attempt at justification merely proclaims a special kind of arrogance. Here, for me, we have the reality: brooder house rather than bullring.

What we are left with then are places that inhabit memory more musically than one of poet Walt Whitman's catalogs: North Platte River and South Platte River, Paxton and Sutherland, Roscoe and Ogallala, North Platte and Cozad,

Brule and Big Springs, Tryon and Thune, Stapleton and Broken Bow, even Lincoln and Omaha and Denver—Keith County and Lincoln County and McPherson County, Perkins, Garden, and Scottsbluff—for our acquaintanceship with our Great Plains country was extensive. Home is both finite and expansive when both are shared with the most important persons in one's life. I eventually brought my New England bride to the home country, where she learned to love sunshine and space, and tolerate wind; and my daughters were born there too before we went elsewhere.

My school classmates could not know that I knew them better than they might have imagined and think of them more than they could possibly believe, remember times of greeting and goodbye, remember using the shower room plumbing for chinning contests after football or basketball practice—am reminded of things like this is where a heavy turquoise and silver ring I bought on the Ute reservation during a fast trip in the Chrysler from Salt Lake to Denver was stolen—and of my innocent surprise at the realization that someone I had to know as a student in my school could be a thief. (And this reminds me that I drove a fast trip in that same Chrysler to Scottsbluff with my mother once, briefly getting that beautiful all-blue machine over one hundred miles an hour, just to see if it would go that fast—something important to know for boys of sixteen or seventeen—briefly, for I always seemed to know the difference between adventure and stupidity, as my mother said). But there were pleasant surprises provided by my schoolmates too, like not caring how well or badly I played the piano at parties when we gathered around to sing *I Wonder Who's Kissing Her Now* or *Nature Boy* or *The Tennessee Waltz* from sheet music that everyone seemed to have then, or their surprising me on my sixteenth birthday, driving out to the country to find me settled down in my work clothes, having just come in from the barn. My parents even hinted that I might take one of the young ladies back to town; but I did not do it, assuming she must have had a ride out—besides, town meant a seventeen-mile round trip, using fuel that was always a major expense and that I would use to get to and from school the next day anyway. First sons probably miss many things needlessly for being responsible. She was the first from our class to marry—someone much older, of course, and already farming, as it turned out anyway.

I remember rare visits to see relatives in Lincoln who recalled the old days, a couple of ancient ladies I assume to have been the great-grandmothers, one of whom would have been a Tripple, the other a Reifschneider, and Great-uncle George, Grandpa Mike's brother, and his family who always lived in the same, big white house, and cousin Bob who showed me how to navigate the University of Nebraska's gymnasium when my basketball team got to go to the state's championship games. I never saw Bob or George's family again after the games, though years later I heard that Bob had become an aeronautical engineer with a family of his own and lives in Dayton, Ohio—which seems eerily appropriate as the place of the Wright brothers beginnings. Uncle George worked for the Union Pacific through times of labor troubles and had to carry a pistol, according to one family legend. The connections have long been broken—not so the memories.

The cemetery at Paxton is south of town on a north-facing slope. On Memorial Day it is surrounded with flags and filled with real and artificial bloom. There are trees now. It is enough above town so that looking north you can see across the new interstate highway, which replaces and parallels the old Lincoln Highway, one on one side of the South Platte, one on the other. From there you can see the river and over the river to the Union Pacific railway and beyond the railway to the elevator, lumber yard, and town. Most of the names on the granite memorials are familiar. My parents and my grandparents are there, most of my aunts and uncles, the first child of my Uncle Roger and Aunt Esther, a couple of former classmates. I don't know if anyone is left to place flowers on Memorial Day. This, finally, will be all that's left to celebrate these wonderful human beings who were the environment of my growing up, the most uncommon common folk of my experience, who lived the ordinary, profound pathos which is every human life, with complete awareness and total dignity.

But it is not there that I go to find them. I go somewhere deep inside myself, where they have become a kind of hopeless longing, a rhythm and a music that make up memory, rhythms and music I hear still, and not only at odd moments, but perpetually: wheat in wind; mother singing in the kitchen; my grandfather's violin; my aunts laughter; windmills creaking; calves bawling at weaning time; my uncles' quiet Sunday dinner appraisals of all things earthy and some things political—an endless kaleidoscope of sounds, smells, sights.

I know that at any hardship or disappointment my father's words will come back to me: *Think nothing of it, Dick. Think nothing of it.*

Always—always there are the March mallards muttering overhead, ephemeral and eternal, coming in at dusk—and always I see my father coming up to the house from the wheat field on a warm June evening with a handful of long green stems and swelling heads of grain, smiling, as he shows the new crop to my mother.

Chris and Rosa, May 22, 1929

0-595-34012-1